The
Baby-led
Weaning
Quick & Easy
Recipe Book

The Baby-led Weaning
Quick & Easy
Recipe Book

GILL RAPLEY
& TRACEY MURKETT

Vermilion
LONDON

This book is for all the parents and babies who are helping to spread the word about baby-led weaning.

10 9 8 7 6 5 4 3 2 1

Vermilion, an imprint of Ebury Publishing,
20 Vauxhall Bridge Road,
London SW1V 2SA

Vermilion is part of the Penguin Random House group of companies whose addresses can be found at global.penguinrandomhouse.com

Penguin
Random House
UK

Produced by **Bookworx**
Project editor Jo Godfrey Wood
Project designer Peggy Sadler

Gill Rapley and Tracey Murkett have asserted their right to be identified as the authors of this Work in accordance with the Copyright, Designs and Patents Act 1988

Published in the United Kingdom by Vermilion in 2017

www.penguin.co.uk

A CIP catalogue record for this book is available from the British Library

ISBN 9780091947552

Printed and bound in China by Toppan Leefung

Penguin Random House is committed to a sustainable future for our business, our readers and our planet. This book is made from Forest Stewardship Council® certified paper.

FSC
www.fsc.org
MIX
Paper from
responsible sources
FSC® C018179

Contents

PART 1

Introduction

Baby-led weaning (BLW) is a wonderful way for your baby to share healthy family meals – right from his very first taste of solid food. He will gradually discover what different foods look like and how they feel, smell and taste; he will learn how to hold them, get them to his mouth and chew them – all by feeding himself at the family meal table.

This natural, commonsense approach to introducing solid foods is a hugely rewarding and enjoyable way for babies to move on to family meals. They learn to love good food and it gives them a solid foundation for healthy eating as they grow up. BLW is great for parents, too, because it takes the stress out of introducing solid foods. This book explains why it makes sense, how to get started and what to expect, and then offers delicious everyday recipes to suit the whole family.

Baby-led weaning & family mealtimes

Shared mealtimes can be among the most enjoyable experiences of being a parent and, as more and more families are finding out, the baby-led weaning approach is easier and more fun for babies – and their parents – than conventional weaning. There's no need to spend time and energy preparing special purées or persuading your baby to accept food from a spoon – and there's no need for mealtime battles. Instead, your baby can explore food when he's ready and go at his own pace, meaning that everyone in the family can eat together and enjoy relaxed, stress-free meals.

It's important that the food you share with your baby is as varied and nutritious as possible, so that he can experience a wide range of different flavours and textures and develop a taste for healthy eating. That's where this book comes in. It will help you to prepare a range of dishes, quickly and easily – from simple spicy beans to rice pudding made with coconut milk – providing him with lots of BLW learning opportunities. All the recipes are tasty, nutritious and wholesome. They are easy to follow and quick to prepare, so they'll soon become tried-and-trusted favourites – for all the family.

"Baby-led weaning felt natural and easy, and it was hugely beneficial to our baby."

About this book

This book starts with an overview of what baby-led weaning is and why it appeals to so many parents (and babies). If you're new to this approach, or need a quick reminder of what it involves, you'll find a guide to getting started and what to expect in the early weeks. The basics of a healthy diet are followed by some tips for supporting your baby's developing skills and the golden rules of BLW. If you need more information on baby-led weaning, go to our first book, *Baby-led Weaning, How to help your baby love good food*, which has more detail on both the reasoning behind the approach and the practicalities involved.

Family mealtimes and sharing the same food are at the heart of BLW. Babies are able to copy what everyone else is doing, feel included and enjoy learning about food in a relaxed, social way.

We know that finding time (and energy) for cooking can be a challenge when you have a baby, so all the recipes (starting on page 35) are straightforward and quick to prepare. Some take only a few minutes, while others can be done in stages. We've also put together a list of dishes that freeze well (see pages 182–3), to help you create a store of healthy meals that just need defrosting and heating. Some of these are good for batch-cooking too, saving you even more time on busy days. Providing healthy food to offer your baby when you are out can also be tricky, so we've listed dishes and snacks to make in advance, which are easy to carry without being too messy (see page 181). **Note:** Recipes suitable for freezing are shown with this symbol ❄ on the recipe page; those suitable for taking out are marked with ☀ .

Understanding baby-led weaning

Weaning is the transition from milk-only feeds to family meals. It starts with a baby's first mouthful of solid food and ends with her very last feed of breastmilk or formula. This period, during which her nourishment comes from the breast or bottle as well as family foods, takes at least six months – and for a breastfed child it may last several years. BLW is a way of introducing solid foods that allows babies to progress at their own pace through this important transition. It will offer your baby the opportunity to explore food as soon as she's ready, using fingers (and, later, cutlery) to eat as much or as little as she wants, and cutting down on milk feeds in her own time. She'll join in with family mealtimes, choosing what to eat from the healthy dishes on offer, and learning as she goes, by looking at, touching, smelling and tasting the food, and by copying other family members.

BLW and your growing baby

Baby-led weaning is based on the way most babies develop in their first year. By about six months muscle strength and co-ordination have developed enough to enable them to sit upright, reach out and grab things they are curious about, and take them to their mouth to investigate them. They are also developing the ability to bite and chew, and their immune and digestive systems have matured enough to cope with other foods. The coming together of these different aspects of babies' development – curiosity, strength, co-ordination, digestion and immunity – coincides with the gradual dwindling of their body's stores of some micro-nutrients. This means that, at around the same time they're beginning to need other foods, they're ready, able and more than willing to feed themselves with them. So, while conventional weaning has always included some finger foods from around six months, with BLW all solid foods are offered this way.

"BLW is like their messy play in the beginning – the amount they learn is just incredible."

A positive learning experience

- BLW allows babies to familiarise themselves with food gradually, through looking, touching, smelling and tasting.
- BLW helps to develop babies' fine movements and hand-eye co-ordination.
- BLW allows babies to learn naturally, by experimenting (the only way to discover how to hold a raspberry without squashing it is to try!)
- Being in control of what's happening and feeling trusted to make their own decisions, encourages babies to explore and learn with confidence.
- Food offers a rich variety of learning experiences – even the very best educational toys can't match it.

Healthy outcomes

- BLW babies develop a healthy attitude to food and mealtimes. There's no pressure to eat, so they're free to:
  - try new foods and choose the nutrients they need
  - concentrate on developing new skills and learning about different foods
  - allow their natural appetite regulation to tell them when they've eaten enough
  - look forward to family mealtimes as relaxed social occasions.

  Research suggests that BLW babies:
  - are at less risk of over-eating when they are toddlers
  - gain a liking for healthy foods that stays with them as they grow up.
- Chewing encourages optimal development of the jaw and facial bones, which in turn helps with teeth spacing and speech.
- BLW allows babies to retain breastmilk or formula as the mainstay of their nutrition for as long as they need to.

Benefits for parents

- Mealtime battles and picky eating are less likely to develop with BLW, so eating as a family is more relaxed and enjoyable.
- Sharing the same meal with your baby is easier than preparing separate food (and then spoon-feeding her while your own dinner goes cold!).
- Eating alongside your baby is more fun and rewarding than trying to persuade her to eat, or fighting her instincts to feed herself.

Mealtimes are an opportunity to experiment and discover how things work. 'What happens if I pick this plate up and then... oh!' It's all part of learning about eating.

Most babies require only small amounts of additional nutrients until they are around nine months old, with milk feeds providing the majority of their nourishment – and acting as an effective nutritional 'cushion' – for the rest of the first year. Baby-led weaning allows them to build up their intake of solid food and cut down on milk feeds gradually, at a pace that is right for each individual baby, so their bodies can adjust naturally. Babies born very pre-term, or who have a disability or medical condition, may need additional help or nutritional supplements before they are ready to fully feed themselves. If you are in doubt about the appropriateness of BLW for your baby, consult your health visitor or doctor.

As more and more parents are finding out, being baby-led just feels right. As they approach six months of age, babies instinctively want to explore food and work out how to eat it. This is as normal and natural as the drive to learn how to crawl, walk or talk. They don't need someone else to feed them and they don't need their food to be mashed or puréed; they simply need the opportunity to follow their instincts. Baby-led weaning allows your baby to move on to family food at the right time for her – when she is ready.

Getting started

You'll know that your baby is ready to start handling food when she can sit upright and reach out with both hands (without falling over), and get things to her mouth accurately. Most babies are able to do this by about six months, but for some it will be slightly earlier, or a few weeks later. Of course, whether or not your baby will be ready to *eat* the food straight away is up to her – this is a key difference between BLW and the conventional approach. Here's how to help her to begin discovering what food has to offer:

When to start
★ Even before she's really ready for solid foods your baby can sit on your lap while you're eating and begin to enjoy the sights, sounds and smells. This is fine – just don't expect her to get food to her mouth (or even to show much interest) until she's at least six months old.

★ Once she wants to start handling food, include her in as many family meals as you can. Choose times when she isn't tired or hungry, so she can concentrate – she's likely to be frustrated and upset if you offer her solid food when what she really needs is the breast or bottle, or a nap. Mealtimes are for learning rather than eating in the early days – breastmilk or formula will satisfy her hunger and nutritional needs.

How to start

★ Sit your baby upright, on your lap or in a highchair, facing the table. Make sure her arms are free and she can reach the food comfortably. Most babies feel more stable if their feet are supported too, rather than dangling.

★ Let her concentrate – don't distract her or try to hurry her while she's handling food. And try to resist wiping her face or hands when she's busy concentrating on eating and learning.

★ It should always be your baby's decision how much she eats – don't try to persuade her to eat more than she wants, or to eat a particular food.

★ Offer her pieces of food by putting them in front of her on the table top or highchair tray or letting her take them from your hand (plates or bowls will be distracting at the beginning, so there's no need to use them if you'd prefer not to). She may want to take things from your plate too, because her instincts tell her that whatever you're eating must be safe.

What to do

★ For the first few months the focus should be on tastes, textures and practising new skills. Offer your baby a few different foods in easy-to-pick-up pieces, so that she can choose what to try.

★ Offer foods that are as nutritious as possible, so that she learns to enjoy, and expect, healthy food and can get all the nutrients she needs.

★ Offer her water with her meals. A shot-sized open cup (see photo, page 23, bottom left) will be small enough for her to pick up easily and better for her jaw development than a sippy cup. If she's breastfed she may prefer to stick to breastmilk – this is fine.

★ Carry on offering breastfeeds or formula as before – your baby will cut these down in her own time.

CAN I COMBINE BLW AND SPOON-FEEDING?

The conventional approach to weaning has always included finger foods from around six months, alongside spoon-feeding. The difference with BLW is that the baby does all the feeding herself and – most importantly – she is trusted to know how fast to eat and when to stop. Giving your baby extra food by spoon-feeding her – either during the meal, after she's finished eating, or at specific mealtimes – takes away this key element of trust, as well as many of the benefits of BLW. It may also teach her to ignore her own appetite and eat more than she really needs. But this doesn't mean that spoons have no place at all in BLW. You'll want your baby to use a spoon (and a fork) eventually, and letting her have a go with a spoon herself, as soon as she's interested, will help her learn. Just so long as she's the one who controls what goes into her mouth.

Managing runny foods

It can be difficult to imagine offering your baby sloppy or runny foods without spoon-feeding her. There are no runny foods that are essential to a baby's diet, but if you want to share something runny with your baby while still allowing her to feed himself, here are some tips:

- Offer smooth foods, like yoghurt, in a small open cup.
- Make porridge or soup extra thick, so it's easy to scoop.
- Offer your baby an edible dipper – such as a piece of celery or a breadstick – and show her how to dip it into the food. She may decide to lick the food off the dipper, or just munch both together.
- Load a spoon with food, then offer it to your baby. She may want to hold it herself or she may prefer to hold your hand to guide it to her mouth.
- Give your baby a spoon that she can hold easily and let her experiment. It may be messy at first but many parents are surprised at how quickly their baby's skills develop.

"When Isabella first got hold of a cucumber stick, she took it towards her face but didn't get it to her mouth. Within a week she could get things to her mouth really well. Now, two or three weeks in she can get smaller things to her mouth and has worked out which end of a piece of broccoli to hold. It's just amazing to watch her skills develop."

When they first start handling food, babies often feel more secure sitting on someone's lap. They are fascinated by what others are eating and are driven by curiosity rather than hunger. They may want to grab the food and sniff, squish or taste it – but they probably won't eat much yet.

Examining, squeezing and tasting food is important for learning how to eat, but it tends to be a messy business – at least at first. If you want to save on the washing, and the room is warm enough, your baby can join in mealtimes in just a nappy.

What to expect

Every baby will approach mealtimes and exploring solid foods in his own unique way, but there are some things that tend to happen with all babies. Here's what you're likely to find:

Mess

There's no getting away from it: introducing solid foods is messy – and BLW can be very messy, at least at first. For babies, squishing, smearing and dropping food are all part of learning and developing new skills. Here are some tips to make the mess easier to manage:

> "Trust your child, enjoy it and embrace the mess; it's worth it for all the benefits he will reap."

★ Plan your baby's bath for after a mealtime, rather than before.
★ Short sleeves and a large, flexible bib can help keep clothes clean.
★ A washable tablecloth or plastic sheet under your baby's chair will allow dropped food to be handed back, as well as protecting the floor.
★ Plain wooden or plastic high chairs are much easier to clean than padded ones. You may prefer a chair that can come right up to the table, rather than having a fixed tray.

A slow start

Don't expect your baby to eat much solid food for the first few months. Most babies don't start eating purposefully until they are nine or ten months old. Many spend a long time just looking at, touching and smelling the food. (Babies' lips and tongues are very sensitive, so you may see lots of licking, too.) Others are keen to taste immediately – and may even bite off a mouthful and chew it – but don't actually swallow anything for several weeks. And then there are some who set off at a cracking pace but seem to lose interest for a month or two. It's also common for babies to want nothing but the breast or bottle for a few days if they are unwell, teething or if something changes in their lives, such as going on holiday or starting nursery. Provided you carry on offering your baby breastmilk or formula whenever he wants, he'll be getting all the nutrition he needs.

Working out how to pick up and hold a variety of shapes, sizes and textures takes practice. These babies are busy refining their pincer grip to help them pick up small pieces of food.

Food fads

Babies sometimes seem to want to binge on a particular food and eat nothing else for days at a time, or they suddenly stop eating a food they previously liked. All of this is normal, and usually short-lived. By staying relaxed and continuing to offer a variety of foods, including those that are currently 'out of favour' as well as those that are 'in', you will help to prevent your baby's occasional food fads from becoming fixed. It's not essential for him to eat something from all the food groups (see pages 28–9) every day; he can balance things out over a week or two – but he will only be able to do this if you keep offering a range of healthy foods for him to choose from.

Gagging

It's very common for babies to gag on foods, whether they're spoon-fed or feeding themselves. The gagging movement is triggered if food touches the sensitive area on the tongue or roof of the mouth before it's ready to be swallowed, or if there is too much to be swallowed safely. Gagging pushes the offending food forward, either out of the mouth, or to where it can be chewed more easily. A baby's gag reflex is more sensitive than an adult's, so gagging is not a sign the baby is in danger – just that he needs to learn to chew food well before moving it back for swallowing – or to bite off slightly less at once. Gagging can be disconcerting to watch but it rarely seems to bother babies, even if they also vomit a little (if anything, gagging is more unpleasant for the baby who is being spoon-fed, because he can't control what's happening). If your baby gags, you don't need to do anything except stay calm and reassure him while he deals with the problem. Don't be surprised if he simply picks the expelled food up and tries again, as if nothing has happened!

"When Milly was about six months there was a bit of gagging when she had long spaghetti. But she seemed happy, so I let her get on with it, and she persevered, slurping it up."

Gagging is sometimes confused with the sort of coughing caused by inhaling food, but this is quite different. Coughing is triggered when food gets drawn too far back in the mouth unexpectedly; it's a reflex to clear the airway and so prevent choking. Provided your baby is sitting upright, he'll usually be able to sort the problem out without any assistance. As with gagging, your role if your baby coughs while eating is to be calm and reassuring. True choking is different again. It occurs when the airway is blocked – and it therefore tends to be silent rather than noisy. It's extremely rare and it requires emergency measures. There is no evidence that choking is any more likely to happen with BLW than with conventional weaning.

Concentration

Exploring solid food is an absorbing experience for babies and it requires concentration. Don't be surprised if your baby frowns at the food rather than smiles at it. He may become frustrated occasionally, if the food doesn't behave as he wants it to. This is no different from what happens when he's trying to master any new skill, such as crawling or walking. It's all part of his learning, and frustration will get less as his skills develop.

BLW SAFETY RULES

- ✪ Make sure your baby is sitting upright to eat – not slumping or lying back. Support around the hips may help him to stay centred (a rolled-up towel if he's in a high chair, or your hands if he's on your lap).
- ✪ Don't let anyone except your baby put food into his mouth (watch out for helpful toddlers!).
- ✪ Don't offer foods that are an obvious choking risk. Cut small round fruits, such as grapes, plums and cherries in half and remove any stones. Remove small bones, gristle and skin from meat (including sausages) and avoid nuts (except ground or as a paste).
- ✪ Let your baby concentrate – don't distract him or try to hurry him while he's handling his food.
- ✪ Never leave your baby alone with food.
- ✪ Explain these rules to anyone else who is looking after your baby (childminder, nanny, friend or relative).

Babies learn an enormous amount when they have the freedom to explore food with no pressure to eat. These babies are totally absorbed in making new discoveries; they'll eat when they're ready.

BLW and your baby's development

Babies' self-feeding skills develop rapidly during the first year or so of handling solid food, at a unique pace for each baby. From working out the co-ordination needed to hold food and gnaw it, to eventually getting the hang of forks and spoons, your baby's learning depends on having the opportunity to try new things, plus plenty of time to practise. Offering her foods that she can manage, alongside some that challenge her, will give her the chance to gain confidence with her existing skills while she works on new ones.

This table explains what developmental milestones to expect at approximately what age and suggests ideas for which foods to offer to help your baby make the most of her abilities as she learns to feed herself.

AGE	ABILITY	WHAT TO OFFER
From around 6–8 months	**Reach and grasp with palmar grip** At first, your baby will use her whole hand to grab food – but she won't be able to open her fist to get at what's inside it. She needs the food to be cut into long pieces (or, like a broccoli floret, to have a built-in 'handle'), so she can hold on to one end while she looks at, pokes and gnaws the other.	**Sticks and strips** Large stick-shaped pieces of food. A good size to aim for is around 5cm/2in long and 1–2cm/½–¾in wide. **To try:** Home-made meat patties or burgers, strips of tender meat, fruit and lightly cooked vegetables (soft enough to bite easily), fingers of toast, well-cooked omelette, large pasta shapes.
From around 7–9 months	**Fist opening and closing** Your baby will start to grab fistfuls of soft food and push or squeeze it into her mouth, and she'll be getting better at holding on to slippery things. She may want to try a dipper (see page 16) and she'll probably be doing more biting and chewing, so she may enjoy crunchier food.	**Sticks and strips,** as above, plus: **soft food in clumps,** such as minced meat, sticky rice, porridge; **slippery foods,** such as large pasta shapes with sauce; **smaller soft foods,** such as strawberries, and **crunchier foods,** such as raw peppers and bread sticks. **To try:** Sticks of celery and other edible dippers, with runny foods like hummus or yoghurt.

AGE	ABILITY	WHAT TO OFFER
From around 8–10 months	**Using fingers** Your baby will be beginning to pick up food with her fingers rather than her whole hand, and will be more adept at using both hands together. She'll be getting the hang of a dipper and she may want to try using cutlery.	All the food types already listed in this table, plus smaller pieces such as rice, peas and raisins. **To try:** Small chunks to have a go at spearing with a fork, and runny food to dip into with a spoon.
From around 9–12 months	**Refined pincer grip** Your baby will begin to pick up very small pieces of food (such as grains of rice and crumbs) between her thumb and forefinger. Many parents notice that this coincides with their baby starting to eat more purposefully and to experiment less with food.	Pretty much everything – aim for a range of healthy foods in a variety of shapes and textures.
From around 11–14 months	**Using cutlery** Your baby may be keen to practise with cutlery, probably finding stabbing with a fork easier than scooping with a spoon, at first. Don't be surprised if she often goes back to using her fingers for quite a while yet.	Any healthy food, remembering to include a variety of shapes, textures, tastes and colours.

Golden rules as your baby grows

The experience of BLW will continue to have benefits long after your baby has started exploring food, especially if you remember these few golden rules:

★ Continue to share healthy foods with your baby.

★ Offer, don't give: let your child decide what to eat from the food you provide. Let her decide how much food she has and how fast she eats.

★ Keep meals as varied as possible and try not to make too much of the foods she loves or hates, so her preferences remain broad.

★ Avoid making eating an emotional issue by turning sweet foods into 'treats' or using them to bribe your child to eat other foods, or to behave in a certain way.

★ Keep mealtimes relaxed and enjoyable.

Babies use trial and error to work out the best way of holding pieces of food. It may not be the way we would do it but this baby clearly has a sense of achievement.

Ensuring a healthy diet

A balanced diet maximises the health of bones, teeth, skin, blood and internal organs, as well as the immune and digestive systems and the development of the brain. It also provides energy and enables growth.

Different foods – even within the same group – contain different vitamins and minerals (see table on page 29). One of the best ways to ensure your baby has a healthy diet is to offer variety – for example, fruit and vegetables in a range of colours, as well as different types of grains and protein foods. This will help to ensure she gets all the micro-nutrients she needs. There are also some foods that it's important to avoid or at least keep to a minimum, for example, salt (see page 32) and sugar, junk food and ready-meals, under-cooked eggs, honey and certain types of fish – see the table on page 33 for more information.

It's quite possible your baby won't like all the foods that you like – but it's equally possible that she'll enjoy things you actively dislike and tend to avoid. Don't be afraid to branch out of your comfort zone occasionally, just to give her a broader eating experience. Her likes and dislikes may turn out to be different from yours longterm. Focusing on keeping things varied will also help you to avoid relying on the same old favourites, which can quickly make mealtimes predictable and less enjoyable, as well as potentially limiting the nutrition available. The more tastes and textures your baby experiences in her first year or so the better the chances that she will continue to eat well throughout childhood and beyond.

What about allergies?
Unless one of the baby's parents or siblings has a confirmed food allergy there is normally no need to delay the introduction of any particular foods and there's no need to introduce one food at a time 'just in case'. Current research suggests that exposure to a wide range of different foods, in small amounts, from the beginning of weaning, may be the best way to prevent allergies. If you are concerned about the risk of allergies, consult your doctor or health visitor, a nutritionist or a dietitian.

Guide to healthy foods

This table lists the main food groups and why each one is needed. It tells you which foods are the best sources for each type of nutrient and offers some tips to help you provide your baby – and the rest of the family – with a healthy and nutritious diet.

Nutrient	Needed for	Good food sources	Tips
Proteins	Growth and repair of all body tissues, structures and organs.	Meat and poultry, fish, eggs, dairy products, nuts, grains (e.g. oats, wheat, quinoa) and pulses (e.g. peas, beans, peanuts, lentils).	Eat pulses and grains together for the best balance of non-animal protein.
Fats	Healthy functioning of brain and nerves, as well as being an important source of energy, especially for children.	**Saturated fats:** dairy products (whole milk, cream, butter and cheese), eggs, meat and poultry. **Mono-unsaturated fats:** avocados, nuts (especially hazel nuts), olive oil and rapeseed oil, eggs, meat and poultry. **Polyunsaturated fats (omega 3 and 6):** nuts (especially walnuts), seeds and seed and nut oils (e.g. sunflower, flax, sesame).	Babies need more of each type of fat than adults, so go for full-fat rather than 'low-fat' options. Avoid hydrogenated and trans fats, found in processed foods, because they carry health risks (see table on page 33).
Carbohydrates	Energy, for body and brain, and to help the breakdown of proteins and to fight toxins.	Fresh fruits, rice, bread and pasta, oats, sweet corn, quinoa, couscous, potatoes and sweet potatoes.	Less highly processed and more complex carbohydrates – in whole grains, pasta, pulses, fruits and vegetables – are more nutritious and release energy more slowly than refined and processed carbs, such as white flour, sugar and white rice. Carbohydrates that release energy slowly (sometimes known as low glycaemic index or low GI carbohydrates) tend to help us feel fuller for longer.

Guide to healthy foods continued

Nutrient	Needed for	Good food sources	Tips
Vitamins	Overall healthy condition and functioning of all body cells and systems: eyes, skin, bones, brain, nerves, blood, digestion and immunity.	**Vitamin A:** carrots, apricots, peaches, watermelon, green veg, liver, full-fat dairy foods. **Vitamin B group:** meat, fish, nuts, eggs, dairy products, wholemeal bread and cereals. **Vitamin C:** fresh fruits/ veg, especially citrus fruits, blackcurrants, strawberries, green vegetables, peppers, potatoes. **Vitamin D:** oily fish (best source), eggs, full-fat and dairy products, meat (and sunlight). **Vitamins E and K:** plentiful in many different foods.	We all need some vitamin C every day but it deteriorates during storage and cooking, so aim to eat foods as fresh and lightly cooked as possible. Whole fruit is a better source of vitamin C than fruit juice, which can contribute to tooth decay. Most of our vitamin D comes from sunlight but that's in short supply in northern European countries, so it's important to make sure we get some in our food.
Minerals	Overall healthy condition and functioning of all body cells and systems, especially blood and bone.	**Iron:** red meat is best source but poultry, eggs, seafood and pulses also contain iron. **Zinc:** tends to occur with iron but is also found in grains, seeds (especially sesame and pumpkin) and lentils. **Calcium:** dairy products (e.g. milk, cheese, yoghurt), the bones of small fish, tofu, hummus, broccoli, sesame seeds, almonds and dark-green leaves. **Trace minerals:** plentiful in a variety of foods.	Children eating foods containing iron, zinc and calcium will generally get all the other minerals they need as well. More iron is absorbed from food if vitamin-C-rich foods are eaten at the same meal. Babies moving on to a vegan diet may need supplements of iron and zinc.
Fibre	Healthy bowel function.	Oats, fruit (especially passion fruit, figs and oranges), veg (especially avocado, Brussels sprouts, sweet potato and beans), chickpeas and tofu.	Babies need some fibre but an excess of very high-fibre foods (see table page 33) is bad for them.

TIPS

Supplements of vitamins A, C and D are recommended for all babies from six months to five years old, and breastfed babies should be given a daily vitamin D supplement from birth. Babies moving on to a vegan diet are likely to need supplements of several vitamins and minerals, including vitamin B12.

Babies love exploring food and being
with their family at the table. Sharing your
baby's enjoyment and keeping mealtimes
relaxed will help build a long-term healthy
relationship with eating.

What to avoid

Part of providing a healthy diet for your baby is knowing what to avoid or limit. Salt is a major concern and the table opposite shows you which other ingredients are bad for babies, why they may be a problem and how to keep them to a minimum.

"Looking back, it's amazing how quickly we got used to cooking without salt – I never use it now."

Salt

Babies' kidneys can't cope with more than 1 gram of salt per day – more than this carries a risk of long-term damage. So excess salt is probably the most important thing to avoid in your baby's diet. This isn't too difficult to do if you make all your food from scratch but you'll still need to watch out for salt when buying ingredients. Lots of everyday foods that are otherwise fairly nutritious, such as ham, cheese, smoked fish, and even bread, can contain surprisingly large amounts of salt, and it's especially high in shop-bought gravies, stocks and sauces.

How to keep your family meals low in salt:
★ Read the labels carefully on all tins, jars and packets, and pick the one with the lowest salt content or none at all. Beware: salt is sometimes listed as 'sodium'; you need to multiply the amount of sodium by 2.5 to get the equivalent amount of salt. For example, 0.5g of sodium is actually 1.25g of salt.
★ Watch out for claims such as 'reduced salt': the amount may simply be reduced compared with a previous version of that food. 'Low salt' can be misleading too, so check the actual amount.
★ Make your own salt-free stock, or buy the lowest-salt version of stock cubes or fresh stock.
★ When you are buying bread, check any labels for salt or ask for the lowest-salt options.
★ Don't add salt when cooking, and limit amounts of flavour-enhancing sauces, such as soy sauce. Adults can add extra to their own food at the table.
★ Choose tinned foods preserved in water or oil rather than in brine (salt water). Rinse tinned and jarred vegetables before using.

★ If your meal includes an unavoidably salty food – such as cheese – offer your baby plenty of vegetables too and some water to drink with the meal. Don't serve more than one salty dish each day.

★ Avoid junk food, take-aways and ready-meals.

★ Check the Salt Watch information in our recipes.

Ingredient	Why it's a problem	Found in	Tips
Added sugar	Sugar provides 'empty' calories, containing no nutrients. It also causes tooth decay.	Sweets, squashes and fizzy drinks, shop-bought cakes, biscuits, breakfast cereals, fruit yoghurts.	Babies often enjoy tart flavours. Watch out for sugar alternatives such as aspartame – less sugar but not a healthy substitute.
Hydrogenated fats and trans-fats	These are not a natural food and they carry health risks.	Some shop-bought biscuits, cakes and pastries. Fried fast foods.	Avoid foods containing partially hydrogenated fat or oil.
Potential infections	Some foods carry a particular risk of food poisoning, which is more serious for babies than for older children/adults.	Honey, undercooked eggs, shellfish, leftover cooked rice.	Avoid honey until your baby is one year. Cook eggs and shellfish thoroughly. Cool leftover rice promptly and refrigerate. Use within 24 hours.
Pollutants (e.g. mercury)	Some pollutants are particularly poisonous to babies and young children.	Certain types of fish, rice drinks.	Avoid shark, swordfish and marlin. Limit oily fish (salmon, trout, mackerel, herring, sardines, fresh tuna) to no more than twice a week.
Artificial additives (e.g. E-numbers, monosodium glutamate (MSG) and sweeteners)	Artificial flavours, colours and sweeteners contain no nutrients and may have harmful side effects.	Fast foods, ready meals, take-aways and junk food such as shop-bought pies, pizzas, burgers, desserts, sweets, squashes and fizzy drinks.	Try to avoid these whenever possible.
Excess fibre	Can irritate the digestive tract of babies and inhibit the absorption of important minerals.	Whole-wheat products, and especially bran.	Offer wholemeal breads and pasta occasionally but avoid anything containing bran.

PART 2

Recipes

Sharing family meals with your baby is great fun – and our range of tasty recipes will mean the food you prepare is delicious and healthy, too. Simple to make and perfect for everyone to enjoy, they'll continue to be family favourites as your child grows up. The variety of dishes will give your baby the opportunity to discover lots of different flavours and textures, providing a great foundation for healthy eating. And because babies' skills develop rapidly in the first few months of BLW, we've selected recipes that can be adapted to suit a range of abilities. You'll find plenty of inspiration for any time of day: whether it's breakfast, a quick lunch, planning ahead for the evening meal, or just a snack to take out or pop into your child's lunchbox.

Note: Recipes suitable for freezing are shown with this symbol ❄ on the recipe page; those suitable for taking out and about are marked with ❄ . 'Serves a family of 4' means two adults and two small children.

Brilliant breakfasts

Many parents feel a bit stumped when it comes to what to offer their baby for breakfast. Maybe you're used to grabbing a croissant and coffee on the way to work, or perhaps you can't see your six-month-old managing the kind of cereals that you have. To start with, many babies want nothing more than a cuddle and a milk feed (whether breastmilk or formula) first thing in the morning. But when your little one does begin to take an interest in something she can get her gums into, these recipes will give you lots of ideas for tasty, wholesome family breakfasts.

This easy, delicious take on traditional eggy bread makes a great start to the day. It can be made with any small, sweet berries, such as strawberries, raspberries and/or blueberries.

Berry eggy bread

Serves 1 adult and 2 small children

Ingredients

▶ 150g/5oz ripe berries (fresh, or previously frozen, defrosted/drained)
▶ 4 slices bread
▶ 1 large egg, beaten
▶ 15g/½oz unsalted butter, for frying

SALT WATCH!

Bread can contain surprising amounts of salt – choose salt-free or lowest-salt options. (See pp. 32–3.)

Method

1 Cut or slice any larger fruits so that they are not too bulky. Lay out the four slices of bread on a board. Arrange half the fruit on one slice of bread and the rest on a second. Lay the remaining two slices of bread on top of the fruit, so you form two sandwiches, with the fruit as the filling. Press down a little on each sandwich to help it stick together.

2 Pour the beaten egg onto a plate and lay each sandwich in the egg, first on one side and then on the other, allowing it to sit for a minute so that the bread absorbs the egg.

3 Meanwhile, heat a large frying pan over a medium to high heat. When the pan is hot, add the butter and swirl it around to melt. Add the sandwiches and cook for around 2 minutes on each side until they're a rich brown.

4 Once both sides are browned, the berry eggy bread is ready to eat. Allow to cool a little and cut into slices for your baby.

This is a very simple, nutritious breakfast that takes just a couple of minutes to make. Add a salad on the side for a light lunch. The omelette is fairly firm and easy to cut into triangles or strips for your baby to pick up. It's good eaten plain but adding extra ingredients means you can introduce your baby to different flavours and textures without having to think up a whole new breakfast.

Golden omelette

Serves 1 adult, 1 small child and 1 baby

Ingredients

- 4 large eggs, beaten
- Freshly ground black pepper (optional)
- Tiny knob of unsalted butter

Suggested optional additions:

- 30g/1oz firm cheese, grated
- 2 small mushrooms, thinly sliced
- A few thin slices of peeled red onion

"Ethan loves strips of thick omelette. But he picks out any mushrooms – maybe it's the texture."

Method

1 Whisk the eggs well, then stir in the black pepper (if using) and any additional ingredients.

2 Take a medium-sized frying pan, around 20cm/8in diameter, and pre-heat over a high heat. When the pan is hot, but not smoking, remove it from the heat. Add the butter and swirl around the pan to melt. Pour in the egg mixture and return to the heat.

3 Swirl the egg around, tilting the pan to ensure that any liquid egg on the top of the omelette runs to the edges and solidifies. When the omelette looks fairly solid, lift up an edge to check the colour. Once it is a light golden brown on the underside, flip it over, using a plate if needed, and cook for another minute or two, until both sides are golden brown.

4 Cut into quarters, triangles or strips to serve.

These fritters make a quick savoury breakfast. They're delicious on their own but when served with sour cream or guacamole they're a great way to give your baby some practice at dipping.

Sweetcorn fritters

Makes 8 fritters – enough for 1 adult, 1 child and 1 baby

Ingredients

- 50g/2oz self-raising flour
- 1 large egg, beaten
- 1 x 195g/7oz tin sweetcorn (no added salt or sugar), drained and rinsed
- Freshly ground black pepper (optional)
- 1–2 tbsp oil, for frying

Method

1 Put the flour into a mixing bowl. Add the egg and whisk well to form a thick batter. Stir in the drained sweetcorn kernels and black pepper (if using). Mix well.

2 If you want a smoother texture, pour the batter into a food processor and whizz for a minute or two to crush the kernels.

3 Heat 1 teaspoon of the oil in a large non-stick frying pan on a medium to high heat. When the pan is hot, pour 1 tablespoon of batter into the pan for each fritter. It should be possible to cook around four fritters at a time. Let them cook for around 2 minutes on each side, until golden brown, then remove them from the pan. Add a little more oil and cook the remaining batter in two or three batches.

To serve

Serve warm or cold, perhaps with some sour cream or Simple guacamole (see page 112), with the fritters cut into halves or quarters for your baby.

These pancakes make a delicious breakfast and are really quick to cook – especially if you make the batter the night before and leave it (covered) in the fridge. They are good served on their own or with some banana slices, or maybe (for adults and older children) with a little maple syrup drizzled on top.

Fluffy blueberry mini-pancakes

Serves a family of 4

Ingredients
- 170g/6oz self-raising flour
- 225ml/8fl oz whole milk
- 1 large egg, beaten
- 50g/2oz fresh, ripe blueberries
- 25g/1oz unsalted butter, for cooking

TIP
You can serve any leftover pancakes cold and they also keep well in the fridge, wrapped in clingfilm.

"We fold pancakes and cut them into soldiers. Even when Sam squashes them they don't disintegrate."

Method

1 Put the flour, milk and egg into a mixing bowl and whisk together until smooth and evenly combined. Stir in the blueberries.

2 Place a large non-stick frying pan over a medium heat. When the pan is warm, but not hot, add half the butter. As it melts, swirl it over the bottom of the pan.

3 For each pancake, pour a tablespoon of batter into the warmed pan. You should be able to fit about 4 spoonfuls into the pan at a time. Cook the mini-pancakes for around 2 minutes, until the undersides are golden brown and bubbles are appearing on the surface of the batter. Then flip them and cook them on the other side. Serve warm, maybe cut into strips for your baby.

If you like porridge for breakfast and want to share it with your baby, you can make an extra-thick version that may be easier for her to handle. But if the thought of the possible mess is too much first thing in the morning, these soft, fruity porridge fingers may be the answer. They make a delicious, easy breakfast and they're very portable, too, so they're great as a snack on the go. A batch will keep for five days in a sealed container.

Fruity porridge fingers

Makes 10 porridge fingers

Ingredients

- 150g/5oz porridge oats
- 50g/2oz plain flour
- 1 tsp ground cinnamon
- 100g/4oz sultanas or mixed dried fruits, such as cranberries, cherries or chopped apricots
- 315ml/11½ fl oz whole milk
- 1 egg, beaten
- 1 large banana, mashed well

Method

1 Preheat the oven to 180°C/350°F/Gas Mark 4 and line a 20cm/8in-square baking tray with non-stick baking paper.

2 Put the oats, flour, cinnamon and dried fruit into a large mixing bowl and stir to mix. Put the milk, egg and banana into a jug and whisk well. Pour into the oat mixture and stir to combine all the ingredients.

3 Transfer the mixture to the prepared tray and bake for 25–35 minutes until fairly firm and lightly browned. (This isn't a flapjack, so it won't go very brown.)

4 Remove from the oven and transfer to a wire ck to cool before cutting. Cut into fingers and serve cold.

This makes a great breakfast (or even dessert) with yoghurt or pancakes, or just on its own. It will keep for three days in the fridge.

Poached fruit salad

Serves a family of 4

Ingredients

- ▶ 100g/4oz natural dried apple rings
- ▶ 100g/4oz natural dried apricots
- ▶ 150ml/5fl oz pure apple juice
- ▶ ½ tsp ground cinnamon (or 1 cinnamon stick)
- ▶ ½ tsp vanilla extract

Method

1 Put all the ingredients into a saucepan and stir well. Cover and simmer gently over a medium heat for 10–15 minutes until the fruit has plumped up and absorbed most of the juice.

2 Remove the cinnamon stick (if used) before serving. Serve warm or cold.

One of the easiest breakfasts ever, this recipe includes a couple of simple textures for your baby to explore. Don't be surprised if she squishes the banana out to play with before eating it!

Banana pitta pockets

Serves 1 adult and 1 baby

Ingredients
- 1 large pitta bread
- 1 large, ripe banana, mashed

Method

1 Warm the pitta bread under the grill (it will puff up slightly), then tear or slice it open around the edge.

2 Spread the mashed banana over the inside, then fold the pitta back together and cut it widthways into fingers. Serve while still warm.

"Jack loves fruit – he gets so excited. He bangs the tray as soon as he sees banana, avocado or strawberries."

Really fast mains

Babies love to explore new tastes and textures at mealtimes, but busy mums and dads rarely have the time and energy in their day to prepare complicated meals for the family. The following recipes are simple and take hardly any time at all to prepare – perfect for those days when you need good food, fast.

This is an easy vegetarian stir-fry, full of chunky vegetables for your baby to explore. A stir-fry is a super-quick way to cook a variety of interesting foods in one go while maintaining the individual flavours of the ingredients.

Tofu stir-fry

Serves a family of 4

Ingredients

- 4 tsp oil, for frying
- 1 x 396g/14oz pack fresh tofu, drained and cut into 2cm/¾in cubes
- 2 cloves garlic, peeled and crushed
- 2 tsp fresh ginger, grated
- 500g/1lb 2oz mixed vegetables – either a combination of mange tout, beansprouts and sliced mushrooms, or pre-prepared stir-fry vegetable mix
- 3 tsp lowest-salt soy sauce

SALT WATCH!

Soy and sweet chilli sauces are salty, so don't add extra to your baby's helping. (See pp. 32–3.)

Method

1 Pour half the oil into a large non-stick pan or wok and heat over a medium heat. Add the tofu pieces and stir-fry, turning frequently, until lightly browned. Remove from the pan and set aside.

2 Add the remaining oil to the pan and return it to the heat. Add the garlic and ginger and stir-fry for just a minute or two, before adding the vegetables. Stir-fry for around 5 minutes until the vegetables have softened. The vegetables will release water as they cook, but if the pan seems dry at any point, just add 2–3 tablespoons of water, which will stop the vegetables from sticking or browning.

3 Once the vegetables are tender, add the browned tofu and soy sauce, stir well.

To serve
Serve with plain rice (boiled or steamed).

This is a very simple dish that's great for when your baby is developing his pincer grip, because it gives him lots of different beans to practise on. If you are serving it with rice, it takes roughly the same time to prepare as it does for the rice to cook. It's also good accompanied by No-salt flatbread (see page 154).

Simple spicy beans

Serves a family of 4

Ingredients

- ▸ 2 tbsp oil, for frying
- ▸ 2 medium red onions, peeled and sliced
- ▸ 1 x 400g/14oz tin mixed beans, drained and rinsed
- ▸ 1 heaped tsp mild curry powder
- ▸ ½ x 400g/14oz tin chopped tomatoes (with no added salt)
- ▸ 2 tbsp water

Method

1 Heat the oil in a large frying pan over a medium heat. Add the onions and cook for 5 minutes until translucent, without letting them brown.

2 Add the beans and curry powder and cook for just a minute before adding the tomatoes and water. Cook for a further 3–5 minutes to allow the sauce to thicken.

To serve

Serve with plain rice (boiled or steamed) or a flatbread such as naan, chapatti or No-salt flatbread (see page 154).

"I can see Nate developing in front of my eyes as he tries to pick the beans up one by one."

These tasty burgers take just minutes to put together. They can be prepared in advance and stored in the fridge, covered, for up to 24 hours.

Pork and apple burgers

Makes 8 small burgers or 16 mini-burgers – enough for a family of 4

Ingredients

- 500g/1lb 2oz minced pork
- 1 medium white onion, peeled
- 1 large or 2 small eating apple(s), cored (and peeled, if you wish)
- 2 cloves garlic, crushed
- Freshly ground black pepper (optional)
- 2 tbsp oil, for frying

TIP

These can be made as regular-sized burgers, cut in half or quarters, which may be easier for little hands to manage.

Method

1 Put the mince into a large mixing bowl. Pull the meat apart and crumble it. Grate the onion and apple into the bowl with the pork. Add the garlic and black pepper (if using). Mix well to combine the ingredients.

2 Pinch off evenly sized pieces of the mixture and form into round burgers, about 2cm/¾in thick. Press each one between your hands to ensure they hold their shape (flouring or wetting your hands will help to stop burgers sticking).

3 When you're ready to cook, heat the oil in a large non-stick frying pan on a medium to high heat. Add the burgers and cook for 5–7 minutes each side, depending on thickness.

4 When the burgers are a golden caramel colour on both sides, check there is no pinkness in the centre. If any pink colour remains, cook them a little longer.

To serve

Serve with some sweet potato fries and crudités, or in a soft bun.

This is a quick and easy version of macaroni cheese that's made in around 15 minutes (but if you have more time and want a crunchier topping see the Variation for an extended option). It can be made with any pasta shapes, so choose whatever your baby can manage. Any leftovers will keep in the fridge for up to three days and can be re-heated before serving.

Hob-top macaroni cheese

Serves a family of 4–6, generously

Ingredients
- 400g/14oz macaroni or large pasta shapes, to suit your baby

For the cheese sauce
- 50g/2oz unsalted butter
- 50g/2oz plain flour
- 700ml/1¼ pints milk
- 150g/6oz mature Cheddar cheese, grated
- Freshly ground black pepper (optional)

Variation
For a crunchy topping, keep back some of the cheese, transfer the finished pasta and sauce to a warmed 30cm x 20cm/12in x 8in baking dish. Sprinkle the rest of the cheese on top, along with some dried breadcrumbs, and bake in the oven at 180°C/350°F/Gas Mark 4 for 25–30 minutes, until the topping is golden brown.

Method

1 Fill a large saucepan with boiling water from the kettle. Bring back to the boil on the hob, then add the macaroni or pasta and cook according to pack instructions. Drain the pasta well once cooked.

2 Meanwhile, make the cheese sauce. In a large saucepan, melt the butter on a gentle heat. When all of the butter is melted, add the flour and stir it in quickly using a wooden spoon to form a thick paste. Continue to stir vigorously for the next couple of minutes until the flour and butter paste bubbles.

3 Pour in a little milk and, using a whisk, mix until the sauce is smooth and beginning to bubble. Then add a little more milk and whisk again. Continue to add more milk each time the mixture begins to bubble, making sure you keep whisking continuously.

4 When all the milk has been added, the sauce should look smooth and glossy. Add the cheese and stir. Season with black pepper (if using) and let it bubble gently for 4–5 minutes. Keep stirring continuously.

5 Once the pasta is cooked and drained, put it back into the saucepan it was cooked in (making sure the pan is dry first), pour in the cheese sauce and stir well. It will appear quite runny at first but will quickly thicken as it cools. Make sure your baby's portion is not too hot for him to touch.

To serve
Serve with a selection of vegetables.

SALT WATCH!

Although it's a good source of protein and calcium, most cheese has a fairly high salt content so it's best not to offer your baby more than one cheese (or otherwise salty) dish on the same day. (See pp. 32–3.)

This dish is very gently spiced, making it a good introduction to some new flavours. The chicken can be prepared in advance and stored in the fridge for up to 24 hours.

Chicken and pepper wraps

Serves a family of 4

Ingredients

- 3 skinless chicken breasts
- 1 tsp paprika
- ½ tsp ground cumin
- Juice ½ lime
- 4 tsp olive oil
- 2 red peppers, deseeded and cut into thin slices, or to suit your baby
- 1 small red onion, peeled and thinly sliced, or to suit your baby
- 4 thin No-salt flatbreads (see p.154)

Method

1 Slice the chicken breasts into strips and put them in a bowl. Add the paprika, cumin, lime juice and half the olive oil. (If you are not making the wraps straight away, cover the bowl and refrigerate until later.)

2 Heat the remaining oil in a large frying pan. Add the peppers and onion and stir-fry on a medium to high heat for 5 minutes. Add the chicken and all the juices and stir-fry for a further 10 minutes, until the chicken is thoroughly cooked.

3 Put some of the chicken mixture on each flatbread and serve immediately.

To serve

Serve with some Simple guacamole (see page 112), sour cream or salsa and perhaps a little grated cheese.

"Ali used to suck on chicken and spit bits out but now he bites pieces and chews them, even with no teeth."

This is a gorgeous sweet curry that offers lots of delicious chunks without too much sauce, making it easier for your baby to get hold of the different shapes. It takes just minutes to make.

Sweet banana curry

Serves a family of 4

Ingredients

- ▶ 2 tsp oil, for frying
- ▶ 1 large red onion, peeled and thinly sliced
- ▶ 1 large eating apple, cored and cut to suit your baby (remove the peel if you like)
- ▶ 2 tsp mild curry powder
- ▶ 4 tsp sultanas
- ▶ 3 large bananas, sliced
- ▶ 150ml/5fl oz water
- ▶ 4 tsp chopped fresh coriander leaves (optional)

Method

1 Heat the oil in a large non-stick frying pan over a moderate heat. Once the oil is warm, add the onion and stir-fry for 5 minutes until soft and fragrant.

2 Add the apple and curry powder. Fry for just a minute to cook the spices, then add the sultanas, bananas and water. Cook for another 3–5 minutes until the fruit has softened and the sultanas have plumped up a little.

To serve

Scatter the coriander on top and serve with some plain rice (boiled or steamed) or a flatbread such as naan, chapatti or No-salt flatbread (see page 154).

"I wasn't sure how Jude would react to spicy food but he enjoys it more than plain dishes."

These fish fingers are an ideal shape and size for babies to pick up and, if you make your own breadcrumbs, they avoid the additives in commercial versions. Choose a firm fish, such as cod, haddock or pollack. Frozen fish works well, too – defrost fully before preparing.

Crunchy fish fingers

Makes 10–15 fish fingers – enough for a family of 4

Ingredients

- 3 tbsp plain flour
- 2 large eggs, beaten
- 100g/4oz fine breadcrumbs (preferably home-made, see Tips)
- 350g/12oz fish, cut into thick strips, about 2cm/1in wide and 5cm/2in long
- A little oil, for frying

TIPS

To make your own breadcrumbs, crumble or grate some slightly stale bread and toast it lightly under the grill. If you prefer to use shop-bought breadcrumbs, go for those with the lowest salt content and avoid artificial colours.

Older children may enjoy helping to dip the fish in the egg or the breadcrumbs.

Method

1 Set out four large plates: the flour on one, the egg on the second, the breadcrumbs on the third. The fourth is for the prepared fish fingers.

2 Take each strip of fish and roll it in the flour to lightly coat it. Shake off any excess, before dipping it in the egg, then in the breadcrumbs. Place the prepared fish fingers on the final plate.

3 Once all the fish fingers are prepared, take a large frying pan and pour in the oil to cover the base to a depth of around 0.5cm/¼in. Heat the oil over a moderate to high heat. Once the oil is hot, add the fish fingers and fry for 4–5 minutes on each side, until crispy and golden brown. Cook them in 2 or 3 batches to avoid crowding the pan. Transfer the cooked fish fingers to a plate lined with kitchen towel, to blot off excess oil. Keep them warm for up to 20 minutes in a 100°C/210°F/Gas Mark 1 oven.

To serve

Serve warm, with some potatoes and vegetables of your choice.

These are delicious, lightly spiced, soft and sweet falafel. They make a healthy meal or snack and are ideal for picnics as they can be eaten warm or cold. You may want to cut the falafels in half to make them easier for your baby to grasp.

Sweet potato falafel

Makes 12–15 falafel – enough for a family of 4

Ingredients

- 2 large sweet potatoes, pre-baked in their skins (45–60 mins at 180°C/350°F/ Gas Mark 4)
- 125g/4½oz gram or chickpea flour
- 2 cloves garlic, peeled and crushed
- 1 tsp ground cumin
- 1 tsp coriander seeds, ground
- 1 tbsp lemon juice
- 1 tbsp chopped fresh coriander (optional)
- Freshly ground black pepper (optional)

Method

1 Preheat the oven to 180°C/350°F/Gas Mark 4. Cover a large baking tray with a sheet of non-stick baking paper and set aside.

2 Slit open the cooked potatoes and scoop out the flesh into a large mixing bowl, discarding the skins. Add the remaining ingredients and mash well to form a smooth paste.

3 Scoop up evenly sized portions and roll the mixture into balls, roughly golf-ball sized, and put them on the baking tray (flouring or wetting your hands will help to stop the mixture sticking). Bake for 15–20 minutes until firm and lightly crisp around the edges.

To serve

Serve warm or cold, perhaps with some White bean and red pepper dip (see page 75). They are particularly good with hummus and sticks of cucumber, red pepper or celery.

TIPS

If you want a milder flavour, halve the spices.

If you don't have any pre-baked sweet potato allow time to cook them beforehand.

This salad makes a delicious, healthy lunch, with different textures and shapes for your baby to explore. The dressing will make the salad a little slippery, so you may want to offer your baby some plain pieces alongside some with dressing.

Chunky Niçoise salad

Serves 1 adult and 1 baby

Ingredients
- 3 small waxy potatoes
- 1 egg, hard-boiled
- 50g/2oz green beans
- ½ 150g/5oz tin tuna (in water), drained, or 1 fillet cooked salmon, or 1 cooked chicken breast, sliced thinly
- 6 cherry tomatoes, halved
- 5 pitted black olives, rinsed and halved

For the dressing (optional):
- 2 tbsp olive oil
- 1 tsp red wine vinegar
- Freshly ground black pepper (optional)

Variation
If you prefer, you can make this recipe using pre-cooked potatoes and beans and a pre-boiled egg.

SALT WATCH!
Choose tuna tinned in fresh water, and olives preserved in oil, rather than brine. (See pp.32–3.)

Method
1 Put the potatoes into a saucepan of cold water and bring to the boil. Cook for 10 minutes, then add the beans and cook for a further 5 minutes, or until the beans are tender. Drain well and leave to cool.

2 Cut the cooled, boiled potatoes into quarters and put them in a large bowl. Peel the egg, cut into quarters lengthways and add to the bowl. Then add the tuna, salmon or chicken, cooked green beans, tomatoes and olives. Mix.

3 To make the dressing, put oil, vinegar and black pepper into a bowl. Whisk together.

4 Immediately before serving, remove a portion of salad for your baby, then drizzle the dressing over the rest and stir gently until all the ingredients are evenly coated. Alternatively, serve the dressing separately.

This is a very popular pasta dish that is delicious warm or cold. It also makes an easy lunch to take out. Penne or farfalle work well in this recipe, but choose whichever pasta shape your baby manages best.

Creamy ham & pea pasta

Serves a family of 4, generously

Ingredients

- ▶ 300g/11oz pasta shapes, to suit your baby
- ▶ 150g/5oz peas (fresh or frozen)
- ▶ 150ml/5fl oz double cream
- ▶ 100g/4oz ham, torn into strips

SALT WATCH!

Ham tends to be quite salty, so make sure your baby is offered plenty of peas and pasta. (See pp.32–3.)

Method

1 Cook the pasta in boiling water, according to the packet instructions. Five minutes before the cooking time is up, add the peas.

2 Drain the cooked pasta and peas. Add the cream and ham and stir until evenly combined. Serve warm or cold.

"I noticed Jack developing his pincer grip when he picked pasta pieces out of his bib pocket."

This simple salad is delicious, and it's great to take out on a picnic. While your baby may not be able to manage the couscous at first, he will enjoy practising – and the broccoli and mackerel will be fairly easy to pick up.

Mackerel, broccoli & couscous salad

Serves a family of 4

Ingredients

- ▸ 100g/4oz couscous
- ▸ ½ small head broccoli, cut into florets, with a generous 'handle'
- ▸ 1 fillet smoked mackerel, skin and bones removed, flaked
- ▸ 75g/3oz dried apricots, cut into chunks to suit your baby
- ▸ 2 handfuls rocket leaves
- ▸ 2 tsp olive oil

SALT WATCH!

Smoked mackerel is often quite salty, so there's just one fillet in this recipe – serve with extra mackerel for adults, if you prefer. (See pp.32–3.)

Method

1 Cook the couscous according to pack instructions.

2 While the couscous is cooking, boil or steam the broccoli until tender. Once cooked, drain and set aside to cool.

3 Once the couscous and broccoli are both cool, transfer them to a large mixing bowl. Add the mackerel, apricots, rocket and olive oil. Stir together until evenly combined and serve.

Frittata makes a nutritious lunch and travels fairly well as a snack or part of a picnic if you pre-cut it and wrap it as separate chunks or slices. A soft, mild and creamy goat's cheese is the best cheese to use.

Spinach & goat's cheese frittata

Serves 1 adult, 1 small child and 1 baby

Ingredients

▶ 100g/4oz frozen chopped spinach, defrosted, drained
▶ 6 large eggs
▶ 50g/2oz goat's cheese
▶ Freshly ground black pepper (optional)
▶ Grated nutmeg (optional)
▶ 25g/1oz unsalted butter

Variation

You can add a variety of cooked vegetables to the frittata mixture, such as potatoes, peppers, green beans or mushrooms.

SALT WATCH!

Although it's a good source of protein and calcium, most cheese has a fairly high salt content so it's best not to offer your baby more than one cheese (or otherwise salty) dish on the same day. (See pp.32–3.)

Method

1 Drain the frozen spinach well, ensuring you have extracted as much water as you can – put it in a sieve over a bowl and press out any excess water using the back of a spoon.

2 Crack the eggs into a bowl and whisk well. Crumble in the goat's cheese and spinach and add black pepper and nutmeg (if using).

3 Put the butter into a medium-sized frying pan and melt over a medium heat. As it melts, swirl it around to cover the base of the pan. Then pour in the beaten egg mixture.

4 Allow the frittata to cook for 3 minutes or so on a medium heat. Run a spatula around the edge to ensure it does not stick. Watch the temperature doesn't get too hot or the frittata will burn on the bottom.

5 When there is only a small amount of liquid egg left on the top, turn the frittata over very carefully. The easiest way is to put a large plate over the pan (using oven gloves to cover both hands), then flip the frittata over quickly onto the plate. Slide it back into the pan, cooked side up, and cook on the second side.

6 After a further 2 minutes, check that no liquid egg remains by cutting into the centre of the frittata with a sharp knife. If it's not properly set, allow it to cook for a further minute and check again.

To serve
Serve warm or cool, cut into slices, maybe with a salad on the side.

... TIP ...
This frittata will keep for two days in the fridge, wrapped in cling film.

These goujons are nice and chunky for babies to pick up and they make a great family meal. The dipping and coating stages are fun for older children to help with.

Chicken goujons

Makes 15–20 goujons – enough for a family of 4

Ingredients

- 3 tbsp plain flour
- 2 large eggs, beaten
- 100g/3½ oz fine breadcrumbs (preferably home-made – see Tip)
- 350g/12oz skinless chicken breast fillets, cut into thin strips
- A little oil, for frying

TIP

It's easy to make your own breadcrumbs by crumbling or grating some slightly stale bread and toasting it lightly under the grill. If you prefer to use shop-bought breadcrumbs, choose those with the lowest salt content and go for a natural colour rather than 'golden' varieties.

Method

1 Set out four large plates. Put the flour on one, the beaten egg on the second and the breadcrumbs on the third. The fourth is for the prepared goujons.

2 Take each chicken strip and roll it around in the flour to lightly coat it. Shake off any excess before dipping the goujon in the egg, then in the breadcrumbs. Place the prepared goujons on the final plate.

3 Once all the goujons are prepared, take a large frying pan and pour in enough oil so that the base is covered to a depth of around 0.5cm/¼in. Heat the oil over a moderate to high heat. Once the oil is hot, add the goujons and fry for around 4–5 minutes on each side until crispy and a rich, golden brown. You will need to cook them in 2 or 3 batches to avoid crowding the pan. Cooked goujons can be kept warm on a baking sheet in the oven at around 100°C/210°F/Gas Mark 1 for up to 20 minutes.

To serve

Serve the goujons warm, with vegetables of your choice, sweet potato fries or sautéed potatoes.

These tasty fishcakes are great for using up leftover mashed potato. If you cook a double quantity one day you can make fishcakes the next; if you don't have any cooked potato allow extra time before you start.

Simple salmon fishcakes

Makes 8 fishcakes – enough for a family of 4

Ingredients

For the fishcakes

▸ 450g/1lb fresh salmon, poached (see recipe p.137), cooled and drained

▸ 500g/1lb 2oz boiled potatoes, mashed

▸ 1 spring onion, thinly sliced

▸ 2 tsp chopped fresh parsley

▸ Freshly ground black pepper (optional)

To coat/cook fishcakes

▸ 3 tbsp plain flour

▸ 1 egg, beaten

▸ 75g/3oz dried breadcrumbs (preferably home-made)

▸ 2–3 tbsp oil, for frying

TIPS

Make your own breadcrumbs by crumbling/grating slightly stale bread and toasting it lightly. If you use shop-bought breadcrumbs, check the labels for salt/artificial colouring.

The fishcakes can be wrapped and stored in the fridge for up to 24 hours before cooking.

Method

1 Put the salmon into a bowl, remove the skin and flake the fish with a fork, checking for bones as you go. Add the potato, followed by the spring onions, parsley and black pepper (if using). Mix to combine all ingredients evenly.

2 Divide the mixture into 8 evenly sized pieces and shape into cakes using your hands (flouring or wetting your hands will help to stop the mixture sticking).

3 When you are ready to cook the fishcakes, set out three plates. Put the flour on one, the beaten egg on the second and the breadcrumbs on the third. Dip each fishcake in the flour, then the egg, then the breadcrumbs, ensuring all surfaces are coated. Heat the oil in a large frying pan on moderate heat. Cook the fishcakes for 4–5 minutes on each side, turning them once, until golden brown on both sides. Take care not to move the fishcakes too much while cooking – they are quite fragile.

To serve

Serve warm, with green vegetables or a salad.

On the table in less than 40

When you're not in a rush but still need something healthy and tasty fairly quickly, these tempting recipes tick all the boxes — and they can be on the table for you and your baby (and everyone else in the family) to enjoy in less than 40 minutes.

Babies find noodles fascinating to explore and this tasty dish has lots of easy shapes for younger babies to pick up, too. It has plenty of flavour without being hot, and all the ingredients are lightly cooked in a coconut-milk broth, which makes them extra tender. Don't be surprised if your baby decides to suck the lime!

Coconut chicken noodles

Serves a family of 4

Ingredients

- 2 tsp oil, for frying
- 400g/14oz skinless chicken breast, cut into strips/chunks
- 2–4 tsp Thai green-curry paste
- 1 x 400g/14oz tin full-fat coconut milk
- 300ml/11fl oz no/low-salt chicken stock, hot
- 100g/4oz dried noodles – either egg or rice noodles
- 200g/7oz mixed stir-fry vegetables (e.g. beansprouts, baby corn, French beans, mange tout)
- 1 lime (optional)

SALT WATCH!

If possible, use salt-free, home-made stock. If buying ready-made or cubes, choose the lowest possible salt content. (See pp. 32–3.)

Method

1 Heat the oil in a large saucepan or wok over a moderate heat. Add the chicken and Thai curry paste and stir-fry for 1–2 minutes, turning the chicken pieces frequently and taking care not to let them brown.

2 Pour in the coconut milk and stock. Put the lid on and simmer for 15 minutes.

3 Add the noodles and vegetables. Cook for another 5–6 minutes with the lid on until the noodles and vegetables are tender.

To serve

Serve warm, with some lime wedges to squeeze over everything.

"Food was like a scientific experiment for ages. Ava just loved examining things and licking them."

This simple, tasty recipe makes the chicken very tender and combines some tempting flavours and interesting textures.

Chicken, pesto & tomato bake

Serves 2 adults and 1 baby

Ingredients

- 2 large skinless chicken breasts
- 4 level tsp basil pesto (home-made or lowest-salt brand)
- 1 x 125g/4½oz ball of mozzarella cheese, cut into 4 thick slices
- 4 cherry tomatoes, halved
- Freshly ground black pepper (optional)

SALT WATCH!

If possible, make your own pesto using a low-salt recipe; otherwise look for a brand with the lowest possible salt content. (See pp.32–3.)

Method

1 Preheat the oven to 180°C/350°F/Gas Mark 4. Cut a slit down one side of each chicken fillet.

2 Spread 1 teaspoon of pesto inside each chicken breast. Place a slice of mozzarella inside the slit, followed by the tomatoes. Put the stuffed breasts in an ovenproof dish.

3 Spread another teaspoon of pesto on each chicken breast, sprinkle with black pepper (if using) and top with a slice of mozzarella.

4 Bake for 20–30 minutes, depending on the size of the chicken breasts. The mozzarella should be golden and bubbling. Cut open the thickest bit of chicken to check the meat is no longer pink. If still slightly pink, return to the oven for a further 5 minutes and test again.

To serve

Serve with new potatoes or pasta and salad or roasted vegetables. Check the tomatoes are cool enough to handle before offering to your baby.

These meatballs are full of Middle Eastern-inspired flavours and are great for babies to pick up. If time is likely to be short, they can be prepared in advance and stored in the fridge, covered, for up to 24 hours, until you're ready to cook them.

Lamb koftas

Serves a family of 4

Ingredients

- 500g/1lb 2oz good-quality minced lamb
- 2 cloves garlic, peeled and crushed
- ½ large white Spanish onion, peeled and grated
- 2 tsp garam masala
- Zest of ½ unwaxed lemon
- 2 tsp oil, for frying

"Amy picked up a whole meatball, then started to chomp. She looked like she was having a great time."

Method

1 Put all the ingredients (except the oil) into a large mixing bowl. Stir well to combine. Pinch off evenly sized chunks and roll into balls, roughly golf-ball sized (flouring or wetting your hands will help to stop the mixture sticking).

2 When you're ready to cook the koftas, preheat the oven to 180°C/350°F/Gas Mark 4. Heat the oil in a large frying pan on a medium to high heat. Add the koftas and fry, turning them regularly, until browned all over. This should take around 5 minutes.

3 Tip the koftas out of the pan onto a large baking tray and bake in the oven for a further 20–25 minutes, until the meat is cooked through. Cut one open and check that no pink meat remains. If it does, return the koftas to the oven for a further 5 minutes and test again.

To serve

Serve warm with slices of pitta bread, pepper and cucumber sticks, and perhaps a little yoghurt. Your baby may find the koftas easier to manage if they are cut in half.

This tasty and nutritious dip can be eaten as part of a light lunch or snack and is great for your baby to practise scooping or dipping. Roasting your own red peppers is very simple, but if you don't have time you can buy ready-roasted peppers in a jar. The dip will keep in the fridge for up to five days.

White bean & red pepper dip

Makes enough for 1 adult, 1 small child and 1 baby

Ingredients

- 1 red pepper, whole, or 75g/3oz ready-roasted red peppers, rinsed and chopped
- 1 x 400g/14oz tin cannellini beans (no added salt, drained and rinsed)
- 1 small clove garlic, peeled and crushed or finely chopped
- 2 tsp tahini
- 2 tsp lemon juice
- 4 tsp olive oil
- Freshly ground black pepper (optional)

Variation

You can make a red-pepper hummus by substituting chickpeas for the cannellini beans.

Method

1 To roast the red pepper, preheat the oven to 180°C/350°F/Gas Mark 4. Place the pepper, whole, on a large baking tray covered with non-stick baking paper and put it in the oven (no need for oil or any covering). Roast for 25–30 minutes until the skin blisters a little. Leave to cool. Once cool, tear open the pepper, pull out the stalk, remove all seeds and white membrane and peel off the skin.

2 If using a food processor or blender, cut the pepper flesh into quarters and blend all the ingredients to form a smooth paste. If using a masher, chop the pepper finely, put it into a large bowl with all the other ingredients and mash until smooth.

To serve

Serve with some falafels, slices of No-salt flatbread (see page 154) and sticks of celery, cucumber and red pepper, or as a baked potato or sandwich filling.

Home-made meatballs are easy to make and these ones are as simple as it gets – plus you know what's in them. They're nice and soft and easy to hold, so they can be a good way to offer iron-rich red meat to your baby. If time is likely to be short, they can be prepared in advance and stored in the fridge, covered, for up to 24 hours.

Oven-baked meatballs

Makes around 16 meatballs

Ingredients

- 500g/1lb 2oz good-quality minced beef – around 10% fat
- 1 clove garlic, peeled and crushed
- 1 tsp dried rosemary or thyme
- 1 egg, beaten
- Freshly ground black pepper (optional)
- 1 tsp oil, for frying

Variation

Re-heat the meatballs in some Super-speedy tomato sauce (see page 148) and serve with pasta shapes or spaghetti.

Method

1 Put all the ingredients (except the oil) into a large mixing bowl. Stir well to combine. Pinch off evenly sized pieces of the mixture and form into balls, roughly golf-ball sized (flouring or wetting your hands will help to stop the mixture sticking).

2 When you're ready to cook the meatballs, preheat the oven to 180°C/350°F/Gas Mark 4. Heat the oil in a large frying pan on a medium to high heat. Add the meatballs and fry until browned, turning them regularly. This should take around 5 minutes.

3 Tip the meatballs out on to a large non-stick baking tray and bake in the oven for a further 20–25 minutes, until the meat is cooked through. Cut one open to check that no pink meat remains.

To serve

Serve warm, with rice and salad, crudités or steamed vegetables such as French beans.

This hearty, chunky vegetable stew has plenty of different shapes and flavours for your baby to explore. It can be served as a main dish but it also makes a lovely side serving for meat dishes.

Mediterranean vegetable stew with butter beans

Serves a family of 4, generously

Ingredients

- 2 tbsp olive oil
- 200g/8oz red onions, peeled and thinly sliced
- 500g/1lb 2oz Mediterranean vegetables, cut into large chunks (such as courgette, aubergine, cherry tomato and red or yellow pepper)
- 1 x 400g/13oz tin butter beans (no added salt), drained and rinsed
- 1 x 400g/13oz tin chopped tomatoes (no added salt)
- 250g large flat mushrooms, sliced
- Handful fresh basil
- Freshly ground black pepper (optional)

Method

1 Warm the oil in a very large pan over a medium heat. Add the onions and cook until fragrant. Add the Mediterranean vegetables, mushrooms and butter beans, followed by the tinned tomatoes.

2 Cook over a medium heat for around 20 minutes, stirring occasionally, until the vegetables have softened. Add the basil and black pepper (if using) and cook until everything is tender.

To serve

Serve warm with some crusty bread, or have as a side dish, perhaps with Lamb chops with rosemary (see page 144).

···················· **TIPS** ····················

If you don't have all of the vegetables listed, celery or butternut squash can be used instead.

This dish freezes extremely well and will keep for up to five days in the fridge.

These delicious, mildly spicy meatballs are perfect for BLW, and the ribbons of cucumber will be great fun for your baby to untangle.

Thai chicken balls with cucumber salad

Serves a family of 4

Ingredients

For the balls
- 500g/1lb 2oz minced chicken or turkey
- 2–4 tsp Thai red paste
- 2 tsp oil, for frying

For the salad
- 1 large cucumber
- 1 tsp sweet chilli sauce

Variation
This recipe works equally well with minced turkey or pork.

········ TIPS ··········

The chicken balls can be prepared in advance and refrigerated for up to 24 hours.

Halving the cooked balls may make them easier for your baby to handle.

Method

1 Crumble the minced meat into a large mixing bowl. Add the Thai curry paste. Stir, using a spatula or wooden spoon, or use your hands to work the paste evenly through the meat. Pinch off evenly sized chunks and roll into balls, roughly golf-ball sized.

2 Pour the oil into a large frying pan and warm over moderate heat. Add the chicken balls and cook for 20 minutes until a rich, nut brown on the outside and no pink meat remains inside.

3 While the chicken balls cook, make the salad. Cut the ends off the cucumber. Run a peeler down it to make a thin, wide ribbon. Turn the cucumber slightly, repeat. Work around it until you reach the watery centre core, which you can discard. Place in a bowl. Add the sweet chilli sauce and stir.

To serve
Serve the chicken balls with the cucumber salad and perhaps some plain rice.

SALT WATCH!

Although the amount here is small, sweet chilli sauce does contain salt (and sugar), so you may prefer to serve it separately for the adults. (See pp.32–3.)

This nourishing, lightly spiced dish offers your baby lots of new flavours to explore and plenty of different shapes to get hold of. It's great for batch-cooking and freezing.

Sweet vegetable tagine

Serves a family of 4

Ingredients

- ▸ 2 cloves garlic, peeled and finely chopped
- ▸ 1 x 2.5cm/1in piece fresh ginger, peeled and finely grated
- ▸ 2 tsp oil, for frying
- ▸ 1 tsp ground cumin
- ▸ 2 tsp ground cinnamon
- ▸ 2 tsp tomato purée
- ▸ 1 x 400g/14oz tin chopped tomatoes (no added salt)
- ▸ 1 x 400g/14oz tin chickpeas (no added salt), drained and rinsed
- ▸ 3 red peppers, cut to suit your baby
- ▸ 2 large courgettes, cut to suit your baby
- ▸ Handful sultanas (optional)
- ▸ 200ml/7fl oz no/low-salt vegetable stock, hot
- ▸ 4 tsp lemon juice
- ▸ Freshly ground black pepper (optional)

Method

1 Put the garlic, ginger and oil into a large pan over a moderate heat. Cook briefly, until the garlic and ginger are softened and aromatic. Add the spices and cook for a further minute, stirring continuously.

2 Add the tomato purée, chopped tomatoes, chickpeas, chopped peppers, courgettes and sultanas (if using), then stir all the ingredients together to combine evenly. Add the stock and allow to cook for around 30 minutes or so, stirring every 5 minutes.

3 Check that the vegetables are tender. If not, allow the tagine to cook for another 10 minutes and check again. When cooked, add the lemon juice and black pepper (if using).

To serve

Serve with couscous or some slices of pitta bread.

SALT WATCH!

If possible, use salt-free, home-made stock. If buying ready-made or cubes, choose the lowest possible salt content. (See pp. 32–3)

This is a marvellous curry that can be eaten on its own or with other curries. It has no sauce, so it's not too slippery and the easy-to-grab chunks of potato make it perfect for BLW beginners. It freezes well, too.

Oven-baked spinach & potato curry

Serves a family of 4

Ingredients

- 50g/2oz unsalted butter
- 1 small white onion, peeled and finely chopped
- 2 cloves garlic, peeled and finely chopped
- 1 tsp fresh ginger, grated
- 2 tsp garam masala
- 2 large white, floury potatoes, peeled and cut to suit your baby
- 400g/14oz frozen spinach
- Freshly ground black pepper (optional)

Method

1 Preheat the oven to 180°C/350°F/Gas Mark 4. Put the butter into a large frying pan and melt over a medium heat. Add the onion, garlic and ginger and cook gently for around 5 minutes, until the onion is soft and fragrant. Keep the heat gentle to ensure that none of the ingredients changes colour.

2 Add the garam masala and potatoes and stir well. Transfer the contents of the pan to a large baking dish, stir in the spinach, season with black pepper (if using) and bake for 20–30 minutes until the potato is really tender. If the potato still feels firm but looks as though it's becoming dry, cover with foil and cook for a bit longer.

To serve

Serve with rice or a flatbread such as naan, chapatti or No-salt flatbread (see page 154).

This is a great dish for the barbecue or grill, and the chunks of fish offer an interesting texture for your baby to explore. The fish can be prepared in advance and left to marinate in the fridge for a few hours, or even overnight. If you are using wooden skewers for your kebabs (rather than metal), soak them in cold water for at least an hour before using, so they don't burn.

Fish kebabs

Makes 4 large kebabs

Ingredients
- 400g/13oz salmon fillet, skin and bones removed and cut into large chunks
- 400g/13oz cod fillet, skin and bones removed and cut into large chunks
- Zest and juice of 1 unwaxed lime
- 2 tbsp olive oil
- 1 clove garlic, peeled and finely chopped
- 1 tsp ground cumin
- 1 large red pepper, deseeded and cut into large chunks

Method
1 Put all the ingredients into a large mixing bowl. Stir well and set aside for 10–30 minutes to marinate (or cover and put in the fridge, if preparing in advance).

2 Preheat the grill or barbecue to a medium to high heat. Thread the fish and pepper chunks onto the skewers and cook for 10–15 minutes until the fish is very lightly browned around the edges and flaky to the touch, and the pepper is softened and a little charred.

3 Use a fork to slide the chunks of fish and pepper from the skewer to offer to your baby.

To serve
Serve warm or cold, with a salad and maybe some No-salt flatbread (see page 154) or pitta.

Quick prep,
eat later

The recipes in this section are ideal for when you want to plan ahead. They're not complicated and don't take much time to put together, but most need a while to marinate or cook. Some of the recipes can be completed in stages, so you can fit them into a busy day, while others are perfect for slow-cooking. Meat is especially tender and easy for babies to eat when cooked slowly, and gentle cooking helps richer flavours to develop. Look out for the snowflake symbol on recipes that freeze well – they're perfect for batch-cooking and freezing for another day.

This simple fish pie is delicious. If your baby is still a BLW beginner, he'll probably just taste the fish pie from his fingers as he explores it, so you may want to offer it with some vegetables that are easy to hold.

Easy fish pie

Serves a family of 6, generously

Ingredients

- ▷ 6 large white, floury potatoes, peeled and cut into 2cm/1in cubes
- ▷ 2 tsp oil, for frying
- ▷ 1 onion, peeled and finely chopped
- ▷ 1 carrot, peeled and finely chopped
- ▷ 300ml/11fl oz double cream
- ▷ Juice of 1 lemon
- ▷ 2 tbsp finely chopped flat-leaf parsley
- ▷ Freshly ground black pepper (optional)
- ▷ 100g/4oz frozen spinach, defrosted and drained
- ▷ 450g/1lb fresh haddock or fresh cod fillet, skin and bone removed, sliced into 1cm/½in strips
- ▷ 75g/3oz mature Cheddar or Parmesan cheese, grated
- ▷ 50g/2oz unsalted butter

TIP

This is a great recipe to batch-cook and can be frozen as a whole pie or in individual portions before baking.

Method

1 Preheat the oven to 230°C/450°F/Gas Mark 8. Put the potatoes into a large pan of boiling water, bring back to the boil and boil until tender. Drain once cooked.

2 Meanwhile, heat the oil in a large frying pan. Add the onion and carrot, and fry until the onion has softened, keeping the heat moderate so the onion doesn't burn. Add the cream, lemon juice and parsley and stir well. Season with black pepper (if using). Pour into a large ovenproof dish, around 20cm/8in square. Stir the spinach into the sauce and add the fish.

3 Mash the potatoes with the cheese and butter. Spread over the fish, spinach and sauce. The pie can be frozen at this stage if you are preparing it in advance. Otherwise, bake in the oven for 25–35 minutes until the potato topping is crisp and the filling is bubbling. If you are cooking from frozen, add 15 minutes.

To serve

Serve with peas or, for younger babies, steamed green beans. Make sure your baby's portion is not too hot in the middle before offering.

These nutritious, economical and tasty home-made burgers are a great standby when you haven't got much food in the house. They're quick to make and cook but, for the best results, you'll need to prepare the mixture in the morning and leave it to chill for a few hours in the fridge. This firms it up and makes it much easier to handle later.

Spiced bean burgers

Makes 6 standard-sized burgers or 12 mini-burgers

Ingredients

▶ 1 x 400g/14oz tin of kidney beans, drained and rinsed
▶ 1 small white onion, peeled and finely grated
▶ 1 large carrot, peeled and finely grated
▶ 1 tsp ground cumin
▶ 2 tsp chopped fresh herbs, such as coriander or parsley (optional)
▶ 4 tbsp plain flour
▶ 3 tbsp oil, for frying

TIP

These burgers can be made small, to suit little hands, or you can make them standard-sized and cut them into halves or quarters after cooking.

Method

1 Put the beans, onion, carrot, cumin, herbs (if using) and 1 tablespoon of plain flour into a mixing bowl. Mash together well with a potato-masher or a fork to form a chunky paste.

2 Cover the mixture and refrigerate for at least 4 hours. When you're ready to cook the burgers, put the remaining 3 tablespoons of flour on a large plate. At the same time, heat the oil in a large non-stick frying pan.

3 Divide the burger mixture into 6 or 12 pieces, depending on the size of burger you want to make. Roll each piece of mixture in the flour and pat gently into a burger shape approximately 1.5cm/¾in thick. Shake off any excess flour and fry the burgers for around 4 minutes on each side until they are a rich brown colour.

To serve

Serve warm with lettuce, crudités, a bread roll and maybe some baked potato wedges.

Satisfying and nourishing, this soup requires a little chopping and preparation, but once done it will cook by itself in a pan on the hob, or in a slow-cooker.

Chunky minestrone soup

Serves a family of 4–6

Ingredients

- 1 tbsp oil, for frying
- 1 large onion, peeled and sliced
- 3 cloves garlic, peeled and chopped
- 1 leek, halved lengthways and cut to suit your baby
- 1 large carrot, peeled, halved lengthways and cut to suit your baby
- 2 medium courgettes, cut to suit your baby
- 2 x 400g/14oz tins chopped tomatoes (no added salt)
- 1 x 400g/14oz tin cannellini beans (no added salt), drained and rinsed
- 100g/4oz dried pasta shapes, size/shape to suit your baby
- 1.3 litres/ 2pt 4fl oz no/low-salt chicken/vegetable stock, hot
- Freshly ground black pepper (optional)

Method

1 Heat the oil in a 4-litre pan. Add the onion, garlic and leek and allow to cook over a moderate heat for around 10 minutes until softened and the onion is slightly translucent. Add the carrot and courgette and cook for a further 5 minutes, stirring continuously.

2 Add the tomatoes and beans and stir well, then add the pasta, hot stock and black pepper (if using). Stir and simmer for at least 45 minutes (or about 3 hours in a slow-cooker).

TIP

This recipe makes quite a lot of soup, but it will keep for up to three days, covered in the fridge, or it can be frozen.

SALT WATCH!

If possible, use salt-free, home-made stock. If buying ready-made or cubes, choose the lowest possible salt content. (See pp.32–3.)

This hearty stew is full of flavour and perfect for cold winter evenings. It's a complete meal in one but is also good with green vegetables or some fresh, crusty bread for dipping. It's very simple to make and works really well cooked in a slow-cooker. It's an ideal recipe to batch-cook and freeze in large or small portions.

One-pot beef stew

❄️

Serves a family of 6, generously

Ingredients

- ▶ 1 tbsp oil, for frying
- ▶ 450g/1lb stewing beef chunks, fat removed
- ▶ 2 large white onions, peeled and chopped into chunky pieces
- ▶ 2 cloves garlic, peeled and chopped
- ▶ 2 large carrots, peeled and cut to suit your baby
- ▶ 2 leeks, halved lengthways and cut to suit your baby
- ▶ 200g/7oz mushrooms, in large pieces
- ▶ 2 large white floury potatoes, peeled and cut to suit your baby
- ▶ 1 x 400g/14oz tin chopped tomatoes (no added salt)
- ▶ 300ml/11fl oz no/low-salt beef or chicken stock, hot
- ▶ 1 sprig fresh rosemary (optional)
- ▶ Freshly ground black pepper (optional)

Method

1 Heat the oil in a large saucepan over a high heat. Add the beef and brown it quickly, stirring constantly, to seal it. This should take around 5 minutes. Add the onions and garlic and cook for a further 3–4 minutes.

2 Add the rest of the ingredients, stir well, cover and cook slowly (so the mixture is just bubbling) for 3 hours on the hob top, or 3–4 hours in a slow-cooker, until the meat is meltingly tender.

To serve

Serve with a green vegetable, such as green beans or sugar-snap peas.

SALT WATCH!

If possible, use salt-free, home-made stock. If buying ready-made or cubes, choose the lowest possible salt content. (See pp.32–3.)

This is a very easy curry recipe with a relatively small number of ingredients. It's a great recipe to prepare in advance and slow-cook throughout the day. It freezes and reheats very well, so if there are only three of you, you can serve half straight away and freeze the rest for another time.

Oven-baked lamb curry

Serves a family of 6

Ingredients

- ▸ 1 tbsp oil, for frying
- ▸ 1 large white onion, peeled and finely chopped
- ▸ 2 cloves garlic, peeled and finely chopped
- ▸ 1 tbsp fresh ginger, peeled and grated
- ▸ 450g/1lb lamb chunks (leg or shoulder)
- ▸ 1 tsp garam masala
- ▸ 1 tsp ground cumin
- ▸ 1 x 400g/14oz tin tomatoes (no added salt)
- ▸ 1 x 400ml/14fl oz tin full-fat coconut milk
- ▸ 250g/9oz frozen spinach

Method

1 Preheat the oven to 180°C/350°F/Gas Mark 4. Heat the oil in a large frying pan. Add the onion, garlic and ginger and fry for 3–4 minutes until fragrant. Add the lamb and stir-fry, turning frequently, to brown the chunks on all sides. Add the garam masala and cumin, followed by the tomatoes and coconut milk.

2 Transfer the mixture to a large oven-proof dish, stir in the spinach and bake for at least 45 minutes, until the lamb is tender and the sauce has thickened. Alternatively, cook in a slow-cooker for 2–4 hours.

To serve

Serve with rice or a flatbread such as naan, chapatti or No-salt flatbread (see page 154).

"I love to see Kasper get in there and really enjoy lots of different sorts of food with us."

Paneer is a mild, firm Indian cheese that soaks up flavours and has a distinctive chewy texture that may be interesting for your baby. You'll get a richer, spicier taste the longer you leave it to marinate.

Paneer kebabs

Makes 4 large kebabs

Ingredients

- 100ml/4fl oz Greek yoghurt
- 1 tsp fresh ginger, grated
- 3 cloves garlic, peeled and finely chopped
- ½ tsp chilli powder
- 1 tsp ground cumin
- 1 tsp garam masala
- Juice of 1 lemon
- 3 tbsp olive oil
- 225g/8oz paneer cheese, cut into 2cm/1in cubes
- 2 red onion, peeled and cut into large chunks
- 1 each red, green and yellow peppers, deseeded and cut into large chunks

SALT WATCH!

Most paneer cheese is not salty, but it's always a good idea to check labels. (See pp.32–3.)

Method

1 Put the yoghurt, ginger, garlic, chilli, cumin, garam masala, lemon juice and oil into a bowl and stir together. Add the paneer, onion and peppers – and stir. Cover and leave to marinate in the fridge for at least 3 hours.

2 When you're ready to cook, preheat the grill to a high setting. Thread the chunks of paneer, onion and pepper onto a skewer and grill, turning regularly, for around 20 minutes, until the paneer is a rich brown colour and the vegetables are tender.

3 Allow the paneer and vegetables to cool, remove from the skewers and serve.

To serve
Serve with rice or grilled meats.

TIP

If you are planning to use wooden kebab sticks, you'll need to soak them in cold water for at least an hour to stop them burning as the kebabs cook. If you don't have any wooden sticks, metal skewers will work just as well.

These drumsticks are mild but full of flavour. Many jerk marinades contain sugar, so this one is a good alternative. Most babies love chicken drumsticks – they are easy to get hold of and the meat is nice and soft. Leaving the drumsticks to marinate overnight will intensify the flavour. Serve with rice and peas or kidney beans, or a salad.

Jerk chicken drumsticks

Makes 8 drumsticks – enough for a family of 4

Ingredients
▶ 8 chicken drumsticks, with skin on

For the jerk marinade:
▶ 2 tsp ground allspice
▶ 2 tbsp maple syrup
▶ 1 clove garlic, peeled and crushed
▶ 2 tsp fresh ginger, grated
▶ 2 spring onions, thinly sliced
▶ 1 tsp olive oil
▶ Pinch chilli powder (optional)

Method

1 Put all the marinade ingredients into a bowl and stir well to combine. Add the chicken drumsticks and stir well, so that each one is evenly coated. Alternatively, you can put the marinade and drumsticks into a large freezer bag, seal the open end and roll the drumsticks around in the marinade. Leave to marinate in the fridge for at least an hour, or overnight.

2 When you are ready to cook the drumsticks, preheat the oven to 180°C/350°F/Gas Mark 4. Lift the drumsticks on to a large non-stick baking tray and discard excess marinade.

3 Bake the drumsticks for 20–30 minutes until the chicken is cooked through and the juices run clear. Cut open a thick part of the meat to check it's no longer pink. If it is pink, return it to the oven for a further 5 minutes and test again.

4 Remove the skin and check there are no sharp bones before offering a drumstick to your baby.

This easy dish is a delicious combination of chunks of silky aubergine in a sweet tomato sauce, topped with melted, golden mozzarella. It's a great way to broaden your baby's experience of textures and flavours – and it freezes well, too.

Baked aubergines with tomato & mozzarella

Serves a family of 4–6

Ingredients

▶ 2 large aubergines, cut to suit your baby
▶ 1 tbsp olive oil
▶ Freshly ground black pepper (optional)
▶ 1 batch of Super-speedy tomato sauce (see p.148)
▶ 2 x 125g/4½oz balls of mozzarella

"Tom likes to squeeze food, look at his hands to see what he's done and squash food into his mouth."

Method

1 Preheat the oven to 180°C/350°F/Gas Mark 4. Put the aubergine chunks and oil into a large frying pan or wok, preferably non-stick. Season with black pepper (if using) and stir-fry for 5 minutes, until lightly browned – the aubergine will absorb the oil very quickly, so you'll need to keep it moving to stop it sticking. If necessary, add a few more drops of oil.

2 Transfer the aubergine to a large ovenproof dish. Add the tomato sauce and stir well. Tear the mozzarella into large chunks and arrange them evenly on top of the aubergine.

3 Bake for 30–40 minutes until the aubergine is really tender. If the cheese browns quickly but the aubergine is still firm, cover with foil and bake for a further 10 minutes.

To serve

Serve warm, maybe with some green salad or steamed green beans.

This is a delicious slow-cook chilli. Chunks of beef work really well as an alternative to minced beef and, when cooked slowly so they are meltingly soft, are perfect for babies to enjoy – and super-nutritious, too. Any leftovers will freeze very well.

Chunky beef chilli

Serves a family of 4

Ingredients

▷ 1 tbsp oil, for frying
▷ 1 white onion, peeled and chopped
▷ 3 cloves garlic, peeled and finely chopped
▷ 500g/1lb 2oz beef chunks, such as chuck steak
▷ ½ tsp ground cumin
▷ ½ tsp ground coriander
▷ 1 tsp ground cinnamon
▷ Pinch chilli powder
▷ 2 low/no-salt beef stock cubes
▷ 1 x 400g/14oz tin red kidney beans (no added salt), drained and rinsed
▷ 2 x 400g/14oz tins chopped tomatoes (no added salt)
▷ 3 tbsp tomato purée
▷ Freshly ground black pepper (optional)

SALT WATCH!

When buying stock cubes, choose the lowest possible salt content. (See pp.32–3.)

Method

1 Put a large frying pan on a medium heat and add the oil, onion and garlic and cook for 5–10 minutes until softened but not browned. Add the beef and stir-fry, turning frequently, for 10 minutes or so until browned. If any water comes out of the meat, keep cooking until it disappears, before moving on to the next stage.

2 Add the cumin, coriander, cinnamon and chilli powder, and crumble in the stock cubes. Stir well. Add the kidney beans and tomatoes, including the juice in the tin, and finally the tomato purée. Stir well and season with black pepper (if using).

3 Cover and leave the chilli to bubble gently for at least 2 hours until the meat is really tender. Alternatively, cook in a slow-cooker for 2–4 hours.

To serve

Serve with rice, flour tortillas or flatbread (such as No-salt flatbread, see page 154) and some sour cream or Simple guacamole (see page 112).

This delicious casserole makes a nourishing, economical meal. It has plenty of different shapes for your baby to practise his skills on, especially once he is developing his pincer grip. The casserole will keep for up to five days in the fridge and it freezes well.

Lentil casserole

❄️

Serves a family of 6, generously

Ingredients

▸ 2 tbsp oil, for frying

▸ 1 large red onion, peeled and chopped

▸ 3 cloves garlic, peeled and chopped

▸ 1 large carrot, peeled and cut to suit your baby

▸ 400g/14oz cooked lentils, rinsed and drained

▸ 1 x 400g/14oz tin chickpeas (no added salt), drained and rinsed

▸ 1 x 400g/14oz tin tomatoes (no added salt)

▸ 500ml/13fl oz no/low-salt vegetable stock, hot

▸ Freshly ground black pepper (optional)

SALT WATCH!

If possible, use salt-free, home-made stock. If buying ready-made or cubes, choose the lowest possible salt content. (See pp.32–3.)

Method

1 Heat the oil in a large saucepan over a medium heat. Add the onion, garlic and carrot and stir-fry, turning frequently, for 3–5 minutes until fragrant.

2 Add the lentils, chickpeas, tomatoes and stock. Add black pepper (if using), put the lid on and cook for at least an hour, until all ingredients are tender. Alternatively, transfer the mixture to a slow-cooker and cook for 3–4 hours until very soft.

To serve

Serve with a flatbread (such as No-salt flatbread, see page 154) crusty bread or mashed potatoes.

"When Ben wants to eat food that his skills aren't ready for I offer something that's easy for him, too."

This casserole has lots of interesting chunks for your baby to enjoy – tender pieces of chicken, wedges of sweet apples and leeks – all in a fruity, creamy sauce. It can be made in a slow-cooker or in the oven. It's not complicated to put together and the recipe multiplies well, so it's ideal for batch-cooking and freezing.

Creamy chicken, apple & leek casserole

❄

Serves a family of 6, generously

Ingredients

- 40g/1½oz unsalted butter
- 500g/1lb 2oz skinless chicken breast – ideally whole mini fillets, but otherwise in chunks
- 3 eating apples, cores removed and cut into 6 wedges (they can be peeled, too)
- 500g/1lb 2oz leeks, halved lengthways and cut to suit your baby
- 200ml/7fl oz apple juice
- 200ml/7fl oz double cream
- 2 tsp cornflour
- Freshly ground black pepper (optional)

Method

1 Preheat the oven to 160°C/320°F/Gas Mark 3 or set up your slow-cooker.

2 Melt the butter in a large frying pan over a medium heat, then add the chicken. Turn the heat up slightly and fry the chicken for 3–4 minutes until lightly browned. Don't allow the heat to get too high, or the butter and chicken will burn.

3 Transfer the browned chicken to a large, lidded casserole dish or your slow-cooker. Return the frying pan to the heat and add the apples and leeks. Fry these for 3–4 minutes. They won't brown in this time, but they will soften a little. Put them in with the chicken.

4 Return the frying pan to the heat one last time. Add the apple juice and turn the heat up, so the juice simmers gently. Add the cream and whisk in. Add the cornflour and whisk

continuously, to thicken the sauce. When the sauce is bubbling and smooth, season with pepper (if using), then pour it over the chicken, apples and leeks, and cover with a lid.

5 Bake for 2–4 hours, depending on how much time you have and how soft you want the apples and leeks.

To serve
Serve with mashed or baked potatoes, or with bread or toast for dipping.

This simple, nutritious soup is great to dip into with toast or bread, or a spoon if your baby is ready give it a go. If he prefers fishing to dipping just lift out a few chunks before you blend it, to add to his bowl. Allow extra time if you don't have peppers already roasted.

Roasted red pepper & butternut squash soup

Serves a family of 4

Ingredients
- 50g/2oz unsalted butter
- 1 medium onion, peeled and chopped
- 2 cloves garlic, peeled and chopped
- 1 medium butternut squash (825g/1lb 13oz prepared weight), peeled, deseeded and cut to suit your baby
- 3 red peppers, roasted, peeled, deseeded and cut to suit your baby (or 225g/8oz ready-roasted peppers, rinsed well)
- 750ml/25 fl oz no/low-salt vegetable or chicken stock
- ½ tsp ground paprika
- Freshly ground black pepper (optional)

> .... **TIP** ....
> To roast your own red peppers see the recipe for White bean and red pepper dip (see p.75).

Method

1 Melt the butter in a large saucepan. Add the onion and garlic and cook on a moderate heat for 5 minutes until the onion is softened.

2 Add the butternut squash, red pepper, stock, paprika and black pepper (if using). Bring to the boil, then cover and turn down the heat, so the soup is bubbling gently. The butternut squash should be very tender after 45 minutes. Blend until smooth.

To serve
Serve with fingers of toast, Mediterranean soda bread (see page 167), Wholemeal soda bread rolls (see page 152) or flatbread (such as No-salt flatbread, see page 154) for dipping.

> **SALT WATCH!**
> If possible, use salt-free, home-made stock. If buying ready-made or cubes, choose the lowest possible salt content. (See pp.32–3.)

Once you've tasted baked potatoes and cheese cooked this way you'll never go back to the old way again and your baby will love them too.

Twice-baked jackets

Serves a family of 4

Ingredients
- 3 baking potatoes
- 100g/4oz mature Cheddar cheese, grated
- 1 spring onion, sliced thinly
- Freshly ground black pepper (optional)

Variation
Sweet potatoes are also delicious prepared like this, but you'll need to bake them on a baking tray (because they drip) and reduce the initial cooking time to 45–60 minutes.

SALT WATCH!

Although cheese is nutritious it tends to be salty, so it's best to make sure your baby's other meals during the day are as low in salt as possible.
(See pp.32–3.)

Method

1 Preheat the oven to 220°C/430°F/Gas Mark 7. Using a sharp knife, prick each potato well, five or six times, all over. Place the potatoes directly on the oven shelf and bake for around 50–75 minutes, depending on their size.

2 When the potatoes are cooked, the inside should be soft and the skin crisp. Test the largest potato by piercing with a sharp knife. The knife should slip in easily. If it's not quite cooked, bake for a further 10 minutes and re-test.

3 Once the potatoes are cooked, cut them in half and scoop the soft flesh into a bowl, trying not to break the skin. Add half the cheese and the spring onion, season with black pepper (if using) and mix well.

4 Spoon the potato mixture back into the skins. Sprinkle the remaining cheese on top and bake the filled skins for 20 minutes until the cheese has melted and the surface is golden.

To serve
Serve with a salad. Make sure the inside of your baby's potato is cool enough for him to touch.

Minced pork and pasta make a rich and tasty combination. Choose the size and shape of pasta most suitable for your baby – a large pasta shape may be easier for him to hold in the early days.

Pork ragù with pasta

Serves a family of 4–6

Ingredients

- 2 tbsp oil, for frying
- 500g/1lb 2oz minced pork
- 1 white onion, peeled and chopped
- 3 cloves garlic, peeled and chopped
- 1 x 400g/14oz tin tomatoes (no added salt)
- 2 tbsp tomato purée
- 100ml/4fl oz water
- Freshly ground black pepper (optional)
- 300g/11oz pasta (shape/size to suit your baby), to serve

TIP
This ragù freezes well (without the pasta).

Method

1 Put a large frying pan on to a medium heat and add the oil. Add the pork and cook for 10 minutes or so until the meat is browned.

2 Add the onion and garlic to the pork in the pan. Cook for a few minutes until the onion starts to soften.

3 Add the tomatoes, tomato purée and water, season with pepper (if using), cover and leave to bubble gently for at least 45 minutes. Alternatively, you can cook the ragù in a slow-cooker for around 2 hours, which will make it thicker, richer and much darker in colour.

4 When you are almost ready to eat, cook the pasta according to the instructions on the pack. Drain it and put it back in the pan you cooked it in, making sure the pan is dry first. Tip in the ragù and stir to combine it evenly with the pasta.

To serve
Serve warm, with some salad, and maybe a sprinkling of grated cheese.

Risotto is great for babies who can pick up handfuls of soft food because it all sticks together. This version is excellent with cod or haddock – fresh, frozen or smoked (preferably not dyed) – or with salmon.

Baked fish risotto

Serves a family of 4–6

Ingredients

▶ 300g/11oz filleted fish, skin removed and cut into 2cm/1in chunks
▶ 30g/1oz unsalted butter
▶ 1 large leek, thinly sliced
▶ 2 cloves garlic, peeled and finely chopped
▶ 275g/10oz Arborio risotto rice
▶ 875ml/1pt 9fl oz no/low-salt chicken stock, hot
▶ Freshly ground black pepper (optional)

SALT WATCH!

Smoked fish has a stronger flavour than fresh but it tends to be more salty, so it's best used only occasionally. If possible, use salt-free, home-made stock. If buying ready-made or cubes, choose the lowest possible salt content. (See pp.32–3.)

Method

1 Preheat the oven to 180°C/350°F/Gas Mark 4. Check the fish for bones, then place in a shallow ovenproof dish, approximately 30cm x 20cm/12 x 8in).

2 In a large frying pan, melt the butter over a moderate heat. Add the leek and garlic and cook for 5 minutes, until translucent.

3 Add the rice and stir briefly to coat the grains in the melted butter. Add the stock and black pepper (optional) and bring to the boil.

4 Once boiling, transfer the risotto to the baking dish, pouring it over the fish. Bake, uncovered, for 25 minutes. Remove from the oven, stir and cover with foil. Bake for another 10 minutes. Taste to check the rice is cooked.

To serve

Serve warm, maybe topped with a little grated Parmesan cheese, plus some peas, asparagus or spinach.

This is a rich, warming stew, packed with chunks of tender, sweet potato and a rich but lightly spiced tomato and coconut sauce. Babies developing their pincer grip will enjoy picking out the chickpeas, while younger babies will be able to get hold of chunks of tomato and sweet potato. This stew works well cooked in a slow-cooker. It's also great for batch-cooking and freezing.

Sweet potato stew

Serves a family of 6

Ingredients

- ▸ 2 tsp oil, for frying
- ▸ 2 cloves garlic, peeled and finely chopped
- ▸ 2 large sweet potatoes, peeled and cut to suit your baby
- ▸ 2 tsp turmeric
- ▸ 2 tsp ground cumin
- ▸ Pinch cayenne pepper (optional)
- ▸ 1 x 400g/14oz tin chopped tomatoes (no added salt)
- ▸ 1 x 400ml/14fl oz tin full-fat coconut milk
- ▸ 1 x 400g/14oz tin chickpeas (no added salt), drained and rinsed

Method

1 Put the oil and garlic into a large saucepan and cook over a moderate heat for 2–3 minutes until soft. Add the turmeric, cumin and cayenne pepper (if using) and stir-fry for a minute to cook the spices. Add the sweet potato and stir.

2 Add the tomatoes, coconut milk and chickpeas. Cook on a gentle heat for around 45–60 minutes, until the chickpeas are soft. If using a slow-cooker, you can leave the stew to cook for 3–4 hours.

To serve

Serve warm with rice or bread, and a vegetable such as green beans or baby corn.

Sweet potatoes make an excellent topping for cottage pie. This dish is quite soft, so if your baby is just starting on solid foods he'll probably be content to lick some meat and sweet-potato mash from his fingers.

Cottage pie with sweet potato mash

Serves a family of 4–6

Ingredients

For the pie filling:
- 2 tsp oil, for frying
- 2 cloves garlic, peeled and finely chopped
- 500g/1lb 2oz minced beef
- 2 tbsp tomato purée
- 300ml/11fl oz no/low-salt beef or chicken stock, hot
- 2 tsp Worcestershire sauce (optional)
- 1 tsp thyme leaves – dried or fresh
- Freshly ground black pepper (optional)

For the topping:
- 4 large sweet potatoes, peeled and cut into 2cm/1in cubes
- 25g/1oz unsalted butter
- 50g/2oz grated cheese (50% Cheddar, 50% Parmesan is especially nice)

Method

1 Preheat the oven to 180°C/350°F/Gas Mark 4 and put a full kettle on to boil.

2 Put the sweet potatoes in a large saucepan. Cover with boiling water, bring back to the boil and cook until soft, which should take about 15–20 minutes.

3 Meanwhile, prepare the filling. Pour the oil into a large frying pan and heat over a moderate heat. Add the garlic and cook for a couple of minutes until fragrant. Add the beef and brown it, breaking the meat up well. This should take 5–10 minutes.

4 Add the tomato purée, stock, Worcestershire sauce (if using), thyme and black pepper. Stir well and leave to bubble gently, without a lid, for around 15 minutes, until the liquid has reduced by around a third. Then pour into an ovenproof dish, about 20cm/8in square.

5 Once the sweet potato is tender, drain well. Mash with the butter and cheese and spread evenly over the top of the beef mixture. Bake for 25–30 minutes until the topping is lightly browned and the filling is bubbling.

To serve

Serve with Herby roast carrots (see page 111) and some green vegetables, such as mange tout or curly kale.

TIPS

Serving the pie with something that's easy to grasp will help to prevent your baby getting frustrated while he works out how to manage it.

This pie freezes well, in both large and small portions.

SALT WATCH!

If possible, use salt-free, home-made stock. If buying ready-made or cubes, choose the lowest possible salt content. (See pp.32–3.)

On the side

The vegetables, salad or other sides you choose to go with your main dish can make a huge difference to how enjoyable the meal is as a whole. Having a real variety of side dishes gives your baby the chance to get even more practice with different foods and flavours. Here are some ideas to help you ring the changes.

This is a tasty, healthy side dish, which is good served with some roast chicken, chunks of fresh tuna or salmon, or even potato wedges. The green beans are perfect for BLW beginners.

Tomato & garlic green beans

Serves a family of 4

Ingredients

- ▶ 1 tbsp olive oil
- ▶ 2 cloves garlic, peeled and crushed
- ▶ 450g/1lb green beans, topped and tailed if fresh, or frozen
- ▶ 1 x 200g/7oz tin tomatoes (no added salt)
- ▶ Freshly ground black pepper (optional)

Method

1 Put the oil and garlic into a large frying pan and cook gently over a medium heat.

2 Once the garlic smells sweet, add the beans. Fry for a minute and add the tomatoes. Season with black pepper (if using) and cook for 10–15 minutes until the tomato sauce is thickened and the beans are tender. Serve warm or cold.

If you find steamed carrots a bit predictable, try these roasted carrots. They're delicious served with a roast dinner, a pie or a casserole, and they are a perfect shape for a BLW beginner to get hold of.

Herby roast carrots

Serves a family of 4–6

Ingredients

- 12 large carrots, peeled, topped and tailed, halved, and cut into quarters lengthways
- 2 tsp dried thyme
- 3 tbsp olive oil
- Freshly ground black pepper (optional)

Method

1 Preheat the oven to 180°C/350°F/Gas Mark 4.

2 Lay the carrot sticks on a large non-stick baking tray. Sprinkle with the thyme, drizzle over the olive oil and season with black pepper (if using). Roast in the oven for 30–40 minutes until tender. Serve immediately.

This delicious creamy dip makes a tasty companion to Chicken and pepper wraps (see page 54) or Chunky beef chilli (see page 96). It's also good spread on fingers of toast or flatbread (such as No-salt flatbread, see page 154), for breakfast, light lunch, or as part of a picnic.

Simple guacamole

Serves a family of 4

Ingredients

▶ 1 large, ripe avocado, peeled and stone removed
▶ 1 tsp red onion, peeled and finely chopped
▶ 1 tsp fresh coriander leaves, finely chopped
▶ ½ tsp lime juice

Method

1 Put all the ingredients into a bowl. Mash with a fork until the mixture takes on a smooth and even consistency. Serve immediately.

To serve

Serve with fingers of toast or flatbread.

TIP

Guacamole is best eaten immediately because it discolours quickly, especially if not covered. It will keep in the fridge for up to 12 hours

"It's fun watching Anna learn how to dip into hummus and guacamole – she gets it all over her but she loves it."

These kebabs are delicious, colourful and fun. They're good eaten warm but they also work well cold and are easy to take out and about as a snack or part of a picnic .

Roasted vegetable kebabs

Serves a family of 4

Ingredients

- ▶ 1 red, yellow or orange pepper, deseeded and cut into chunks
- ▶ 1 courgette, cut into chunky slices
- ▶ 150g/5oz cherry tomatoes
- ▶ 2 tbsp olive oil

TIP

If you are planning to use wooden kebab sticks, you'll need to soak them in cold water for at least an hour to stop them burning as the kebabs cook. If you don't have wooden sticks, metal skewers work just as well.

Method

1 Preheat the oven to 180°C/350°F/Gas Mark 4. Put all the vegetables into a large mixing bowl. Add the oil and toss everything well, to coat the vegetables in oil.

2 Thread the vegetables onto the sticks, varying the order, and lay the kebabs on a large non-stick baking tray.

3 Bake for 15–20 minutes until the vegetables are tender and lightly charred around the edges. Serve warm or cold.

"Jasmine really loves roasted veg – we take any leftovers out as snacks."

This quick version of broccoli and cauliflower cheese is a great side to serve with a roast dinner or perhaps as a vegetarian main. You won't need to make a traditional cheese sauce – just combine all the ingredients and bake until golden and bubbling.

Broccoli & cauliflower cheese

Serves a family of 4

Ingredients

▸ 750g/1lb 10oz broccoli and cauliflower florets
▸ 400ml/14fl oz crème fraîche
▸ 100g/4oz Cheddar or Gruyère cheese, grated
▸ 1–2 tsp Dijon mustard (optional)
▸ Freshly ground black pepper (optional)

SALT WATCH!

Although a good source of protein and calcium, most cheese is salty, so avoid serving this dish as a side with a main containing salty ingredients. (See pp.32–3.)

Method

1 Preheat the oven to 180°C/350°F/Gas Mark 4. Put all the florets into a large mixing bowl and add the crème fraîche, a third of the grated cheese, and the mustard and black pepper (if using). Stir well, preferably using a spatula, to ensure the florets are well coated in the crème fraîche and all the ingredients are evenly combined.

2 Tip the mixture into a large baking dish, approximately 25cm x 20cm/10in x 8 in. Make it roughly level and sprinkle the remaining cheese over the top.

3 Bake for 30–40 minutes, until the topping is a deep golden brown, the florets are tender when a sharp knife is inserted into the stem, and there is no excess water in the dish.

TIP

You can freeze this dish
before baking, and bake from
frozen (adding on another
10 minutes to the cooking
time), or freeze after baking,
and then re-heat in the oven
or microwave.

These are delicious and make a popular change from ordinary chips – they're healthier too, and perfect for babies who are BLW beginners to grab easily. They're tasy with the skin on, but you can peel them if you prefer.

Baked sweet potato fries

Serves a family of 4–6

Ingredients

▸ 2–3 large sweet potatoes, washed thoroughly

▸ 1–2 tbsp olive oil

▸ Freshly ground black pepper (optional)

"Sweet potatoes are a real winner in our house – both my kids love them!"

Method

1 Preheat the oven to 180°C/350°F/Gas Mark 4. Cut the sweet potatoes into 1–2cm/½–1in thick slices, lengthways. Then cut each slice into chips and place on a large baking sheet.

2 Drizzle the oil over the chips and season with black pepper (if using). Turn the chips so that each piece is lightly coated in oil.

3 Bake for 20–25 minutes until tender and soft inside, but crispy on the outside.

This is an incredibly easy way of cooking rice, with no need for draining or risk of it boiling dry. Pilau rice is a traditional accompaniment for curry.

Oven-baked Pilau rice

Serves 2 adults and a baby

Ingredients
- 10g/½oz unsalted butter
- ½ cinnamon stick
- 3 green cardamom pods
- 3 cloves
- ¼ tsp turmeric
- ½ small onion, peeled and finely chopped
- 125g/4½oz basmati rice, washed
- 200ml/7fl oz no/low-salt chicken stock, hot

SALT WATCH!
If possible, use salt-free, home-made stock. If buying ready-made or cubes, choose the lowest possible salt content. (See pp.32–3.)

"Aurora shovels rice into her mouth in handfuls. She's starting to practise with little bits, too."

Method

1 Preheat the oven to 180°C/350°F/Gas Mark 4. Melt the butter in a saucepan over a gentle heat. Add the spices and let them sizzle for a few seconds, until you can smell the aromas.

2 Add the chopped onion to the pan and cook for 5 minutes or so on a gentle heat, until it starts to soften.

3 Add the rice and stir until all the grains are coated with butter.

4 Add the stock and stir to combine all the ingredients. Transfer the mixture to a 750ml/1¼-pint baking dish, cover with foil, and bake for 20–25 minutes, until the rice is tender. Remove the cinnamon stick and cardamom pods before serving.

These mushrooms make a tasty side dish. They're also delicious served in slices with some buttered-toast fingers. Mushrooms have a unique smell, taste and texture that can help to broaden your baby's range of experience.

Baked mushrooms with lemon & thyme

Serves a family of 4

Ingredients
- 2 large flat mushrooms
- ½ tsp fresh thyme leaves
- ½ tsp lemon juice
- Freshly ground black pepper (optional)

TIP
This dish keeps well in the fridge for 24 hours and can be reheated easily.

Method

1 Preheat the oven to 200°C/390°F/Gas Mark 6. Lay the mushrooms on a baking tray with the stalks pointing upwards. Sprinkle the thyme leaves and lemon juice over the underside of the mushrooms, together with the black pepper (if using).

2 Bake in the oven for 15–20 minutes, until tender. The mushrooms will release plenty of juices as they cook. Serve whole or sliced, with the juices poured on top.

"Mushrooms were some of Maha's first favourite foods – she was fascinated by them."

The flavour of cauliflower becomes beautifully sweet and nutty when it's roasted. It's delicious served with all sorts of dishes, from roast dinners to curries, and it's just as good cold as it is warm.

Roasted cauliflower

Serves a family of 4, generously

Ingredients

- ▶ 1 large head of cauliflower with outer leaves removed, cut into florets (with stalk 'handles' for your baby to grasp)
- ▶ 2 tsp olive oil
- ▶ Freshly ground black pepper (optional)

"Roasting makes veg easier to handle and you can make a whole lot in one go and stick them in the fridge."

Method

1 Preheat the oven to 180°C/350°F/Gas Mark 4. Put the cauliflower florets on a large, non-stick baking tray. Drizzle the olive oil over them and season with black pepper (if using). Roll the florets around in the oil so that each one is very lightly coated.

2 Bake for 20–30 minutes until tender, lightly browned around the edges, and crispy to the touch. The cooking time will depend on the size of the florets and their water content (which can vary). Remove from the oven and serve. Adults may like to sprinkle their portion with a little salt.

One of Spain's most popular tapas, patatas bravas are delicious served with omelette or frittata and they are very easy for babies to handle.

Patatas bravas

Serves a family of 4–6

Ingredients

- 6 tbsp olive oil
- 500g/1lb 2oz waxy potatoes, peeled and cut to suit your baby
- 1 red onion, peeled and finely chopped
- 1 clove garlic, peeled and chopped
- 1 x 400g/14oz tin chopped tomatoes (no added salt)
- Freshly ground black pepper (optional)
- Pinch sweet Spanish paprika (optional)

Method

1 Preheat the oven to 200°C/390°F/Gas Mark 6. Pour 4 tablespoons of the oil into a large ovenproof roasting or baking tray and heat in the oven for 3 minutes until hot. Remove the tray from the oven and place the potato chunks in the tray. Stir them around to ensure each chunk is coated in oil. Bake for 30–45 minutes until browned and crispy.

2 Meanwhile, make the tomato sauce. Pour the remaining 2 tablespoons of oil into a pan. Add the onion and garlic and cook for 5 minutes over a moderate heat so that they soften.

3 Add the tomatoes and black pepper (if using). Then allow the sauce to bubble gently for 20–30 minutes until thickened. Add the paprika (if using). Pre-warm a large plate.

4 Once the potatoes are roasted, spread the tomato sauce on the pre-warmed plate and arrange the potatoes on top, so that they stay crisp. Serve warm.

Croquettes make a delicious side and are a handy way to use up leftover mashed potato. If you don't have any cooked potatoes you will need to allow extra time to peel, cook, mash and cool some before you start. The croquettes can be cooked in a large pan or a deep-fat fryer.

Potato croquettes

Makes Around 20 croquettes – enough for a family of 4–6

Ingredients

- 600g/1lb 5oz white, floury potatoes, peeled, cooked and mashed
- 100g/4oz mature Cheddar cheese, grated
- 3 tbsp plain flour
- 2 large eggs, beaten
- 60g/2½oz dried breadcrumbs
- A little oil, for frying

TIPS

Make your own breadcrumbs by crumbling/grating slightly stale bread and toasting it lightly. If you use shop-bought breadcrumbs, check labels.

Uncooked croquettes can be frozen and cooked straight from the freezer.

Method

1 Put the mashed potato into a large mixing bowl and add the cheese. Stir to combine.

2 Set out four plates. Put the flour on one, the beaten egg on the second and the breadcrumbs on the third. The fourth is for the prepared croquettes.

3 Pinch off balls of potato and roll each one into a thick tube shape, similar to a large cork. Roll each croquette in the flour, then the egg, and finally in the breadcrumbs.

4 When you are ready to cook the croquettes, pour the oil into a large, heavy pan, to a depth of at least 5cm/2in and heat over a moderate heat (or set your electric deep-fat fryer to 160°C/320°F). When the oil is hot, add the croquettes in small batches of around 4–6 at a time. Fry until they reach a rich, nut brown, which should take 2–4 minutes (4–7 minutes if cooking from frozen).

5 Using a slotted spoon, lift the cooked croquettes out of the oil and lay them on a plate lined with a few sheets of kitchen towel, to blot any excess oil.

6 Either serve immediately or transfer to a large baking tray covered with non-stick baking paper and pop them in an oven preheated to 180°C/350°F/Gas Mark 4. They can safely be left to keep warm for up to 15 minutes, while you cook the rest. Serve warm.

Roasted Brussels sprouts are much tastier than the steamed or boiled version, with an enhanced, nutty flavour. They make a perfect addition to a roast dinner and are easy to cook, especially if you have the oven on anyway.

Roasted Brussels sprouts

Serves a family of 4–6

Ingredients

▸ 500g/1lb 2oz Brussels sprouts, stalks trimmed
▸ 2 tsp olive oil
▸ Freshly ground black pepper (optional)

"Mia tries everything – sometimes there's a lemon-face but she always goes back for more."

Method

1 Preheat the oven to 180°C/350°F Gas/Mark 4. Put the sprouts on a large baking tray. Drizzle with the olive oil, season with black pepper (if using) and roll them around to ensure they are all lightly coated in oil. Cover with foil.

2 Roast for 15 minutes and then remove the foil. Cook for a further 5–15 minutes (depending on how large the sprouts are), until tender. Serve warm or cooled. You may need to halve the sprouts so your baby can pick them up easily.

A great alternative to chips made from potatoes, these are firm, crispy sticks of cooked polenta, with a soft inside, which provide an interesting contrast in texture for babies. Search for polenta that looks like grains (not ready-cooked polenta) – it's usually labelled as 'polenta bramata'.

Polenta chips

Makes Approximately 36 fries – enough for a family of 4

Ingredients

- 100g/4oz polenta bramata (coarse corn meal)
- 500ml/1 pint 2fl oz no/low-salt chicken stock, hot
- ½ tsp dried rosemary
- Freshly ground black pepper (optional)
- 30g/1oz Parmesan cheese, finely grated
- 6 tbsp oil, for frying

SALT WATCH!

If possible, use salt-free, home-made stock. If buying ready-made or cubes, choose the lowest possible salt content. (See pp.32–3.)

TIP

You can prepare the polenta in advance and keep it covered and refrigerated in the baking tray for up to 24 hours – until you're ready.

Method

1 Line a baking tray, roughly 12cm x 15cm/6in x 7in square, with baking paper.

2 Put the polenta into a pan with the stock. Cook over a moderate heat for 5 minutes, whisking continuously. The polenta will thicken dramatically. Keep whisking to ensure there are no lumps.

3 Remove from the heat, stir in the rosemary, black pepper (if using) and Parmesan, and pour the mixture into the baking tray. Leave to cool for at least an hour.

4 When you are ready to make the chips, cut the polenta into pieces about 1–2cm/½–1in wide and 5cm/2in long. Heat the oil in a pan, add the polenta chips and fry on all four sides until a rich, golden brown. Once cooked, turn off the heat and allow the chips to cool in the pan for a couple of minutes, to firm up a little.

These soft, sticky discs of sweet potato are excellent served warm as a side or cold as a salad. They go very well with roasted meats and casseroles and take just minutes to prepare before roasting.

Baked sweet potato rounds with orange & thyme

Serves a family of 4–6

Ingredients

- 4 large sweet potatoes, peeled
- Zest and juice of 1 large orange
- 1 tsp olive oil
- 1 tsp fresh or dried thyme leaves

"When Liam has a new food he puts it in his mouth, looks surprised, takes it out, has a look, puts it back and starts to chew."

Method

1 Preheat the oven to 180°C/350°F/Gas Mark 4. Slice the sweet potatoes widthways to form chunky rounds, about 1.5cm/½in thick. Lay the rounds on a large baking tray.

2 Mix together the orange zest and juice, the oil and thyme leaves and pour over the potato rounds. Turn them over so that they are coated on all sides.

3 Cover the tray with baking foil and bake for 20 minutes.

4 After 20 minutes, remove the foil and cook for another 5–15 minutes, until the sweet potato is very tender and the sauce has reduced and become sticky. Serve warm or cold.

This is a very simple stir-fry dish with a light, delicate flavour. Choose stir-fry vegetables in a variety of shapes and sizes (beansprouts, for example), to make the dish really interesting for your baby. This dish goes perfectly with Quick poached salmon (see page 137).

Vegetable stir-fry

Serves a family of 4

Ingredients

- ▸ 2 tbsp sesame oil
- ▸ 3 tsp fresh ginger, grated
- ▸ 400g/14oz pack stir-fry vegetables
- ▸ 1 tsp lowest-salt soy sauce

SALT WATCH!

For those family members who like extra flavour, you can serve additional soy sauce or sweet chilli sauce at the table. However, these sauces are salty so don't add extra to your baby's helping. (See pp.32–33.)

Method

1 Pour the sesame oil into a wok and place over a high heat. Add the ginger paste and stir-fry for just a minute.

2 Add the vegetables and stir-fry for 4–7 minutes, keeping everything moving, until the vegetables are soft and tender. Add the soy sauce and stir through. Serve immediately.

"Elisha loves different shapes to try – she seems to enjoy the challenge of learning how to hold something new."

This is the simplest of potato salads to make and is ideal to take out and about. It doesn't use mayonnaise (which contains raw eggs, making it unsuitable for babies), so all the family can enjoy it.

Potato salad

Serves a family of 4, generously

Ingredients

- ▶ 750g/1lb 10oz new potatoes, whole or halved, depending on size
- ▶ 3 tbsp olive oil
- ▶ Freshly ground black pepper (optional)

Optional dressing:
- ▶ 1 tbsp balsamic vinegar
- ▶ 1 tsp chopped chives or spring onions
- ▶ ½ tsp Dijon mustard
- ▶ ¼ red onion, peeled and finely sliced

TIP

This dish will keep for up to three days in the fridge, in a sealed container.

Method

1 Boil the potatoes until tender. Make the dressing (if using) by mixing the ingredients together.

2 Drain the potatoes well. While they are still hot, transfer to a mixing bowl. Pour the oil over them, then add the black pepper and dressing. This will improve the flavour and texture, as the flavours will be absorbed by the potatoes as they cool. Serve slightly warm, or cold.

"As soon as Charlie sees food now he reaches out to get it, he's so excited."

Super-simple dishes

Babies benefit from being introduced to as many new flavours and textures as possible. That way their experience is fun and varied, they develop broad tastes, and they have the best chance of getting all the nutrients they need. But it's easy to find yourself in a rut when you're cooking for a family. If you don't have the time or energy to come up with new dishes, here are some super-simple recipe ideas that will add variety to your family's meals in no time.

This gently spiced, simple lunch idea will help to broaden your baby's experiences of flavours. Many babies like to dismantle dishes like this and eat the pitta and filling separately, so don't be surprised if this is what your baby decides to do.

Spiced pitta pockets

Serves a family of 2–3

Ingredients

- ▶ 2 tbsp olive oil
- ▶ 1 tsp cumin seeds, ground
- ▶ 1 tsp coriander seeds, ground
- ▶ 1 tsp fennel seeds, ground
- ▶ 1 large courgette, sliced into thick rings (approx. 0.5cm/¼in)
- ▶ 300g/10oz cherry tomatoes
- ▶ 2–3 large pitta breads

SALT WATCH!

Bread can contain surprising amounts of salt – choose salt-free or lowest-salt options. (See pp.32–3.)

Method

1 Heat the oil in a medium-sized non-stick frying pan over a moderate heat and add the ground spices, courgette and tomatoes. Fry gently for around 10 minutes until some of the tomatoes have collapsed and the courgette is tender and lightly browned.

2 Toast the pitta breads, split open and stuff with the courgette and tomatoes. Allow to cool (test the tomatoes – they often stay hotter than the rest) and serve cut into quarters.

To serve

Serve with salad.

TIP

Traditionally, the spices in this recipe are ground in a pestle and mortar but if you don't have one you can use pre-ground cumin and coriander seeds and leave out the fennel seeds (which are hard to buy ready-ground).

This dish makes a great light lunch or snack that you can rustle up in just minutes. The pea mixture also works well as a dip for your baby to practise his dipping or scooping technique.

Creamy pea crostini

Serves 1 adult and 1 baby

Ingredients

- ▶ 100g/4oz frozen peas
- ▶ 1 tbsp mascarpone cheese
- ▶ Freshly ground black pepper (optional)
- ▶ 2–3 slices bread – ciabatta works especially well

TIP

The pea mixture will keep (covered) in the fridge for up to five days.

"When we have something on toast Maryam turns it over and scrapes the topping off with her bottom teeth."

Method

1 Put the peas into a saucepan, with enough water to cover them, and boil for around 5 minutes until tender. Drain well and set aside to cool completely.

2 When the peas are cool, put them in a bowl with the mascarpone and season with black pepper (if using). Mash together well.

3 Just before you are ready to eat, toast the bread until golden. Spread the hot toast with the pea mixture, slice into fingers and serve.

To serve

Serve with salad.

This simple dish is perfect if you are in a hurry, and green beans are a natural finger food for babies. It's also a handy dish to take on picnics.

Pesto pasta with green beans

Serves a family of 4

Ingredients

- 300g/11oz pasta (shape and size to suit your baby)
- 200g/7oz green beans, ends trimmed
- 6–8 level tsp pesto (home-made or lowest-salt brand)

SALT WATCH!

If possible, make your own pesto using a low-salt recipe; otherwise, look for a brand with the lowest possible salt content. (See pp.32–3.)

Method

1 Cook the pasta according to the packet instructions in a large pan of boiling water. Either steam the green beans on their own or add them to the pasta 5 minutes before the cooking time is up, so they can cook together.

2 Once cooked, drain the pasta and green beans. Return them to the pan and stir in the pesto. Serve warm or cold.

"Theo has learnt to open his fist now. He drops the food then picks it up again so the other end pokes out."

English muffins are ideal for making mini pizzas and, because they're chunky but soft, they're easier for babies to hold and bite into than a conventional pizza base.

Muffin pizzas

Serves a family of 4

Ingredients

▶ 3 English muffins
▶ 3–4 tsp tomato purée
▶ 100g/4oz mozzarella cheese, torn into small strips
▶ 1 tsp dried oregano (optional)

SALT WATCH!

English muffins and other breads can contain surprising amounts of salt – choose salt-free or lowest salt options. (See pp.32–3.)

Method

1 Preheat the grill. Split the muffins in half and toast the outsides (with the cut side facing down).

2 When the outsides are lightly toasted, remove the muffins from the grill. Turn them over, spread the untoasted surface with tomato purée and lay the cheese on top. Sprinkle with oregano.

3 Grill for 2–4 minutes until lightly golden brown and bubbling around the edges. Remove from the grill and allow to cool slightly before serving.

"Rory makes a funny face whenever he touches food, and again when it goes in his mouth – even if he really likes it."

Poaching is a very simple way to cook salmon, and it keeps it juicy and soft, which makes it easy for babies to eat. Poached salmon is delicious hot or cold and can be used in a number of recipes, such as Simple salmon fishcakes (see page 67).

Quick poached salmon

Serves a family of 4

Ingredients

▸ 3 fillets fresh, unsmoked salmon
▸ 1 lemon, sliced (optional)
▸ 1 small bunch fresh parsley, thyme or dill (optional)
▸ 1 bunch spring onions, roughly sliced (optional)

"Poached salmon is nice and easy for Josh to break up with his hands and mash up in his mouth."

Method

1 Place the salmon fillets skin side down in a large, deep frying pan. Fill the pan with cold water, so that the salmon is just covered. Add the lemon, herbs and/or spring onion for an extra layer of flavour.

2 Put the pan on the heat and bring the water to the boil. As soon as it boils, turn the heat off. Turn the fish fillets over, cover and leave for 10 minutes, then remove them from the water and dab with kitchen paper to dry. Serve immediately or set aside to cool. Discard the water, lemon and herbs (if used).

To serve

Serve hot or cold with steamed new potatoes or mashed potato, and a Vegetable stir-fry (see page 128) or other vegetables of your choice.

This classic Italian salad is colourful and tasty, and has plenty of different textures for your baby to discover. It doesn't keep for longer than an hour, though, because the mozzarella starts to go watery after that, so it's best to make it just before you want to serve it.

Tricolore salad

Serves a family of 4

Ingredients

- 2–3 large or 300–450g small ripe tomatoes
- 1 x 125g/4½oz ball of mozzarella cheese (preferably Buffalo)
- 2 large, ripe avocados, skin and stone removed

Dressing (optional):

- 4–6 basil leaves
- 3 tsp olive oil
- 3 level tsp pesto (home-made or lowest-salt brand)

Method

1 Slice the tomatoes and put them into a bowl. Tear the mozzarella into small chunks and add to the bowl. Cut the avocado into chunks and add them too. Gently toss everything together.

2 If you want to add a dressing, mix the basil, olive oil and pesto together and drizzle over the salad. Stir gently and serve immediately.

SALT WATCH!

If possible, make your own pesto using a low-salt recipe; otherwise, look for a brand with the lowest possible salt content. (See pp.32–3.)

This classic dish is ideal for babies who are mastering the pincer grip, with lots of pieces that are perfect for little fingers. Be warned, though: if your baby decides to pick up each individual pea and grain of rice, lunch may take a little longer than you'd planned!

Egg fried rice with peas

Serves a family of 4, generously

Ingredients

▸ 175g/6oz basmati rice
▸ 2 tbsp oil, for frying
▸ 2 large eggs, beaten
▸ 100g/4oz peas, cooked
▸ 2 spring onions, thinly sliced

"At first Alice pushed handfuls of rice into her mouth. Once she developed a pincer grip she picked up smaller bits."

Method

1 Cook the rice according to the instructions on the packet. Drain thoroughly and cool quickly until completely cold. (Refrigerate if not using immediately.)

2 Heat the oil in a wok or a large frying pan. Add the cold rice and toss it around for a few seconds, then add the egg. Stir well to ensure the egg is evenly distributed through the rice.

3 Add the peas and spring onions. Continue to stir until the egg is firmly set. Serve immediately. Adults may like to add soy sauce or sea salt to their portion for extra flavour.

Oven-baked drumsticks make an easy meal. They can be cooked in advance to take out as part of a picnic. Drumsticks are easy for BLW beginners to get hold of and your baby will love to gnaw or suck the tender chicken. The lemon and thyme are optional, but they give the chicken a subtle, delicious flavour.

Chicken drumsticks

Makes 8 drumsticks – plenty for a family of 4

Ingredients

- 8 chicken drumsticks, with skin on
- 3 tbsp olive oil
- 1 unwaxed lemon, cut into 4 slices, widthways
- 4 tsp thyme leaves
- Freshly ground black pepper (optional)

Method

1 Preheat the oven to 180°C/350°F/Gas Mark 4. Put the drumsticks on a large non-stick baking tray and drizzle the oil evenly over them. Lay the lemon slices on top and sprinkle with thyme and black pepper (if using).

2 Bake for 20–30 minutes, until the skin is crisp, the chicken juices run clear and no pink meat remains inside. Cut open a thick part of the meat to check – if you see any pink colour, return the drumsticks to the oven for a further 5 minutes and test again.

3 Remove the skin and any thin or sharp bones before offering a drumstick to your baby.

To serve

Serve warm with some salad or roasted vegetables, or cold, as part of a picnic.

This is an easy, nutritious light meal to enjoy at any time of day. Asparagus spears are perfect for little hands to hold and many babies love their unique taste. Older babies (and adults) can use the asparagus to dip into runny egg but the eggs should be hard-boiled for babies under a year old.

Buttered asparagus with boiled eggs

Serves a family of 4

Ingredients

- 1½–2 bunches fresh asparagus, depending on appetite
- 4 large eggs
- 1 large knob unsalted butter

TIP

Babies under 12 months should have their eggs hard-boiled. Offering some runny food, such as hummus, alongside your baby's egg will mean he can dip, along with everyone else.

Method

1 Half-fill two saucepans with boiling water – one large enough to hold the asparagus without it being squashed, plus a smaller one for the eggs. Bring the water in both pans back to the boil. Warm a plate ready for serving.

2 When the water comes back to the boil, add the eggs and the asparagus. Adjust the heat to keep both pans boiling. Cook the eggs for 4–6 minutes (8–10 minutes for hard-boiled) and the asparagus for 3–5 minutes, until tender.

3 Lift out the soft-boiled eggs and put them into egg cups. Drain the asparagus spears and lay them on the warmed plate, with the butter on top, so that it melts onto them. Peel and quarter any hard-boiled eggs for younger babies. Give each person an egg and let them help themselves to the asparagus.

Chops are a delicious way to eat lamb, and rosemary adds a wonderful extra flavour. Younger babies will probably do more sucking or gnawing than actual eating, but they'll enjoy holding the chop and tasting the flavour of the meat juices.

Lamb chops with rosemary

Ingredients

6–8 lamb chops

For the marinade (optional):

▶ 1–2 tsp olive oil
▶ 1 sprig rosemary

> **TIP**
> Lamb chops go very well with a side of Mediterranean vegetable stew with butter beans (see p.77).

Method

1 Rub the olive oil over the chops and place them in a sealed bag with the rosemary. Refrigerate for a couple of hours (or overnight).

2 When you're ready to cook the chops, take them out of the fridge and discard the rosemary. Place a large frying pan over a high heat or pre-heat the grill.

3 When hot, add the lamb chops. Fry or grill for 4–5 minutes on each side, until the surface is a rich brown, the fat has crisped and the meat is cooked through (check by cutting the thickest of the chops in half).

To serve

Serve with a choice of vegetables.

This delicious, simple salad offers three distinct textures for your baby to explore and makes a lovely side dish or light lunch, perhaps with some pitta bread. It will keep (covered) for up to 12 hours in the fridge.

Feta, cucumber & avocado salad

Serves a family of 4

Ingredients

▶ 1 cucumber, cut into chunks to suit your baby

▶ 2 large, ripe avocados, skin and stone removed, cut into chunks to suit your baby

▶ 100g/4oz feta cheese, crumbled

▶ Juice ½ lemon

▶ 2 tsp chopped dill (optional)

SALT WATCH!

Like many cheeses, feta is nutritious but quite salty, so it's important to make sure your baby has plenty of the other ingredients with just a little of the cheese. (See pp.32–3.)

Method

1 Put all the ingredients into a large mixing bowl. Stir gently to combine.

2 Serve (or refrigerate) immediately.

"We had salad in the garden today with some friends. Noah joined in, sucking on different things."

This delicious fish dish is full of protein, and the boneless, buttery chunks are ideal for babies to pick up.

Pan-fried fish with lemon & herb butter

Serves a family of 4, generously

Ingredients

- 4 fillets of white fish, skin on
- 50g/2oz unsalted butter
- Zest of 1 unwaxed lemon
- 2 tsp fresh herbs, such as parsley, basil or dill, chopped
- Freshly ground black pepper (optional)

TIP

This recipe works best with firm white fish, such as cod or haddock, because they break easily into chunks. Flat fish, such as sole, bream or bass, are good once your baby can manage smaller flakes.

Method

1 Ensure the fish fillets are boneless and dry before you start. Pick any visible bones out from the flesh and dry the fillets by patting them with kitchen paper.

2 Melt the butter in a large frying pan over a moderate heat, allowing it to foam. Add the fish, skin side down, and cook for around 3 minutes in the melted butter. Finely grate the lemon zest over the fish. Add the herbs and black pepper (if using).

3 Turn the fish over and cook for another 2–3 minutes. When it's cooked it will be bright white throughout and flake when you try and pull it apart with a fork. If it looks translucent it's still raw, so let it cook for a little longer. Remove the skin and any remaining bones. Serve warm, cut into manageable chunks for your baby.

To serve

Serve with steamed new potatoes and vegetables or salad.

This recipe makes an extremely simple pasta sauce, but it's also incredibly useful as a quick base for lots of different dishes, from bolognaise to chilli, casseroles and curries. It takes just minutes to make and is perfect for batch-cooking and freezing.

Super-speedy tomato sauce

Serves a family of 4

Ingredients

- 1–2 cloves garlic, depending on taste, peeled and finely chopped
- 2 tsp olive oil
- 1 x 400g/14oz tin chopped tomatoes (no added salt)
- Freshly ground black pepper (optional)

···· **TIP** ········

This dish freezes well, so cooking multiple batches at once can save you time later.

Method

1 Put the garlic and oil into a non-stick frying pan and cook over a moderate heat until it smells sweet and aromatic. (Don't allow it to burn or brown or it will taste bitter.)

2 Add the tinned tomatoes with their juice, and cook over a gentle heat until thickened. This should take around 5 minutes. Add the black pepper (if using). Once thickened, the sauce is ready to eat or combine with other ingredients. Allow to cool before freezing.

To serve

Serve warm as a simple sauce, with pasta shapes to suit your baby, maybe with a little Parmesan cheese and torn basil leaves on top. Or use as a base for other dishes, such as Baked aubergine with tomato & mozzarella (see page 94) and Creamy tomato pasta (see opposite).

If you have some Super-speedy tomato sauce (see opposite) already made, this dish is really quick to prepare. It won't take more than the ten or so minutes needed to boil the pasta.

Creamy tomato pasta

Serves a family of 4

Ingredients

- 300g/11oz pasta (shape and size to suit your baby)
- 1 batch of Super-speedy tomato sauce (see opposite)
- 4 tsp mascarpone cheese

Variation

Sardines can be substituted for the mascarpone. Choose sardines in oil (rather than tomato sauce or brine), so they are less salty. Drain them, then mash with a fork and remove any large pieces of bone. Stir into the sauce and heat thoroughly.

Method

1 Cook the pasta according to the packet instructions. Meanwhile, make or reheat the tomato sauce.

2 Once the sauce has thickened, add the mascarpone and stir into the sauce. When the pasta is cooked, drain well and return to the (dry) pan. Add the sauce and stir to combine. Serve warm or cold.

"I loved watching Kai eat pasta and tomato sauce for the first time – it was just everywhere."

Tasty bakes

There's nothing like the smell of something delicious baking in the oven to whet your appetite. From soda bread rolls to healthy flapjacks and muffins, the recipes in this section provide tasty bakes for all your family. And for those days when you are out and about with your baby, there are plenty of snacks that travel well, too.

This simple soda-bread recipe uses home-made buttermilk, making delicious rolls for dipping into soups, stews and sauces. They are also great eaten plain or buttered at any time of the day, and are handy to take out as snacks.

Wholemeal soda-bread rolls

Makes 12 rolls

Ingredients

- ▶ A little oil, for greasing
- ▶ 400ml/14fl oz whole milk
- ▶ 1 tbsp lemon juice
- ▶ 225g/8oz wholemeal self-raising flour
- ▶ 225g/8oz white self-raising flour
- ▶ 1 heaped tsp bicarbonate of soda

TIP

These rolls are at their best the day they are made, but they freeze well and defrost in just a couple of hours.

Method

1 Preheat the oven to 220°C/430°F/Gas Mark 7 and grease a 12-hole silicone or metal muffin tin (or line a metal muffin tin with paper cases).

2 Pour the milk into a jug and add the lemon juice. Leave for 3–5 minutes while you prepare the remaining ingredients. The lemon juice will cause the milk to curdle slightly, creating a buttermilk. (It may look slightly odd but this is supposed to happen!)

3 Sift both flours and the bicarbonate of soda into a large mixing bowl and stir to combine. Pour in the curdled milk and stir well until all the flour is incorporated into the mixture.

4 Spoon the mixture evenly into the muffin tin and bake for 16–22 minutes until risen and lightly browned. The top will feel firm and slightly crusty. Remove from the oven; allow the rolls to cool in the tin for 10 minutes, then transfer them to a wire rack to cool fully.

This deliciously sweet bread can be served plain or toasted and buttered. It's great for taking out and about as a snack, too. Older babies may enjoy picking out the sultanas!

Banana bread

Makes 1 large loaf

Ingredients

- ▶ 3 large ripe bananas, mashed
- ▶ 75ml/3fl oz sunflower oil or 65g/2½oz unsalted butter, melted and cooled
- ▶ 2 eggs, beaten
- ▶ 1 tbsp whole milk
- ▶ 1 tsp vanilla extract
- ▶ 2 tbsp maple syrup
- ▶ 150g/5oz self-raising flour
- ▶ 2 tsp baking powder
- ▶ 75g/3oz sultanas (optional)

TIP

Banana bread is best eaten fresh but it can be frozen.

Method

1 Preheat the oven to 180°C/350°F/Gas Mark 4 and line a 900g/2lb loaf tin with non-stick baking paper.

2 Put the mashed bananas, oil, eggs, milk, vanilla extract and syrup into a bowl and whisk together until evenly combined.

3 Sift the flour and baking powder into a large mixing bowl. Pour in the liquid mixture and stir to combine evenly and incorporate all the flour. Add the sultanas (if using).

4 Pour the batter into the prepared tin and bake for 25–30 minutes until the loaf is golden brown and well risen, and a knife inserted into the centre comes out clean. If any liquid mixture clings to the knife, then return the tin to the oven and bake for another 5 minutes before testing again.

5 Allow to cool for 15–20 minutes in the tin, then turn out on to a wire rack to cool fully before serving.

These delicious soft flatbreads are perfect served warm instead of a naan or chapatti to mop up a curry sauce, or as an alternative to pitta bread, cut into strips, to eat with dips. For a tortilla-style wrap, roll the dough out more thinly before cooking.

No-salt flatbread

Makes 4 large flatbreads

Ingredients

- 275g/10oz strong white bread flour, plus a little extra to flour the work surface
- 1 tsp quick-action dried yeast
- 1 tbsp olive oil
- 180ml/6fl oz warm water

Method

1 Put the flour and yeast into a bowl and mix well. Add the oil and warm water and stir in to form a soft and very sticky dough. Knead on a floured work surface for 5 minutes. Return the dough to the mixing bowl, cover with clingfilm and leave to rise in a warm place for 20 minutes.

2 Flour (or wet) your hands and divide the dough into four or more pieces, depending on the size of your frying pan and how thin you want the bread to be. Knead the first piece lightly on a well-floured work surface and roll out into a circle, up to 0.5cm/¼in thick.

3 Heat a large non-stick pan over a moderate
to high heat. Put the dough circle into the
dry frying pan (no oil needed) and cook for
around 2 minutes on the first side.

4 When the bread starts to blister, flip it over
and cook for another 2 minutes or so on the
other side, until golden brown and puffy. Repeat
with the remaining pieces of dough.

To serve
Serve with salads, dips, a curry or meatballs.

This is a richly fruited, super-simple-to-make cake that contains no added sugar, dairy products or eggs. It is ideal for when your baby is ready to cope with more challenging textures. Fruit loaf keeps extremely well and is ideal for wrapping and taking out as a snack or part of a picnic. It can also be frozen.

Easy fruit loaf

Makes 1 large loaf

Ingredients

- ▶ 200g/7oz sultanas
- ▶ 170g/6oz dried mixed berries
- ▶ 100g/4oz dried apricots, chopped
- ▶ 100g/4oz stoned dates, chopped
- ▶ 350ml/13fl oz pure orange juice
- ▶ 225g/8oz self-raising flour
- ▶ 1 tsp ground cinnamon
- ▶ 75g/3oz ground almonds

Method

1 Preheat the oven to 180°C/350°F/Gas Mark 4 and line a 900g/2lb loaf tin with non-stick baking paper.

2 Put the dried fruits and orange juice into a pan. Warm gently for 5 minutes, so that the juice helps the fruit to plump up, then pour into a large mixing bowl.

3 Add the flour, cinnamon and ground almonds and stir well to form a thick batter. Pour into the prepared loaf tin, level off and bake for 35–45 minutes until the cake is a rich, deep brown and a knife inserted into the centre comes out clean. Test the cake after 35 minutes. If the knife comes out coated in batter, return to the oven for a further 5 minutes and test again.

4 Allow to cool for 15–20 minutes in the tin, then turn out on to a wire rack to cool fully before serving.

These savoury scones make great snacks to take out and about and spinach is a tasty addition to traditional Cheddar scones. They can also be made as mini-scones, which are just right for baby hands.

Cheddar & spinach scones

Makes Approximately 10 standard-sized scones or 24 mini-scones

Ingredients

- 225g/8oz self-raising flour plus a little extra to flour the work surface
- 50g/2oz unsalted butter
- 50g/2oz mature Cheddar, grated, plus a further 25g/1oz as a topping (optional)
- 100g/4oz frozen chopped spinach, defrosted and all excess water squeezed out
- 100ml/5fl oz whole milk

SALT WATCH!

The topping of added cheese is optional because it tends to be salty. You may wish to put topping on some of the scones and reserve those without for your baby. (See pp. 32–3.)

TIP

These scones are best eaten on the day they are made, but they do freeze very well.

Method

1 Preheat the oven to 220°C/430°F/Gas Mark 7 and lightly grease a large baking tray.

2 Put the flour and butter into a large mixing bowl and rub the butter into the flour until it looks like breadcrumbs. Stir in the cheese and spinach and add the milk. Bring the mixture together to form a very soft dough.

3 Turn out on to a well-floured work surface and knead gently to bring the dough together into a soft ball. Roll out to about 2cm/¾in thick and stamp out rounds using a pastry cutter or a glass, 5–6cm/2in for standard-sized scones and 4cm/1½in for mini-scones. Put the rounds on the prepared baking tray. Lightly knead the remaining dough, roll out and cut again, until all the dough is used up.

4 Top some or all of the scones with the extra cheese (if desired) and bake for 12–15 minutes (8–12 minutes for mini-scones), until well risen and golden. Allow to cool thoroughly before eating.

These crustless individual quiches, made in a muffin tin, make an excellent breakfast, lunch or snack and are very quick to prepare. They keep well in the fridge for three to five days and they freeze well, too.

Mini-quiches

Makes 12 quiches

Ingredients
- A little oil or unsalted butter, for greasing
- 4 large eggs, beaten
- 2 tbsp whole milk
- 75g/3oz Cheddar cheese, grated
- 25g/1oz unsalted butter, melted

Optional fillings:
- 50g/2oz shredded fresh spinach leaves
- 50g/2oz sweetcorn kernels (no added salt)
- 50g/2oz cherry tomatoes, chopped
- 50g/2oz frozen peas
- 50g/2oz red, yellow or orange pepper, chopped

Method

1 Preheat the oven to 200°C/390°F/Gas Mark 6 and grease a 12-hole silicone muffin tin (or line a metal muffin tin with paper cases).

2 Put the eggs, milk, cheese and butter into a large mixing bowl and whisk together. Stir in your chosen filling (if any), then pour the mixture into the prepared tin, filling each hole or case to around two-thirds full.

3 Bake for 15 minutes until the quiches are a rich golden brown and are nicely risen.

4 Leave the quiches in the tin for at least 20 minutes (they will sink a little) before turning them out to finish cooling.

TIP
Silicone muffin tins are generally easier to use and clean than metal ones, especially for this recipe. If you don't have a silicone tin, line your metal tin with paper cases. The quiches will be easier to turn out.

Home-made scones are quick and easy to make and they taste great – especially compared with shop-bought versions. They are best enjoyed on the day they're made, but they also freeze very well.

Wholemeal sultana scones

Makes 8 scones

Ingredients

- ▶ 175g/6oz wholemeal self-raising flour
- ▶ 175g/6oz white self-raising flour, plus a small handful extra for flouring the work surface
- ▶ 1 tsp bicarbonate of soda
- ▶ 75g/3oz cold butter, cubed
- ▶ 75g/3oz sultanas
- ▶ 200ml/7fl oz whole milk

TIP

These scones are best made in the suggested size for the ideal balance of crunchy outside and fluffy, soft inside – mini versions don't work quite as well. Simply cut them in half or quarters to offer to your baby.

Method

1 Preheat the oven to 200°C/390°F/Gas Mark 6 and cover a large baking tray with non-stick baking paper.

2 Sift the flours and bicarbonate of soda into a large mixing bowl. Add the butter and rub it in to form a breadcrumb-like mixture. Add the sultanas and stir to distribute through the flour.

3 Pour in the milk and stir well to form a wet dough. Turn out in a ball on a well-floured work surface. Roll the ball of dough generously in the flour, to coat all surfaces and make it easier to handle. Use your hands to flatten the ball into a fat disc, around 2.5cm/1in thick. With a sharp knife cut the dough into 8 evenly sized triangles, dusting the blade in a little flour before each cut to prevent sticking.

4 Lay the triangles on the prepared tray, spaced generously. Bake for 12–16 minutes until the scones are light brown around the edges and feel lighter when lifted than they did before baking. If they still feel heavy, bake for another 2–3 minutes before re-testing. Remove from the oven, cool on a rack and enjoy fresh.

These tasty little biscuits get all their sweetness from the apple juice and sultanas. They keep well in an airtight tin and freeze very well, too, taking just a couple of hours to defrost.

Apple biscuits

Makes 25–30 biscuits

Ingredients

- ▶ 200g/7oz plain flour, plus a little extra to flour the work surface
- ▶ 75g/3oz unsalted butter, cubed
- ▶ 75ml/3fl oz apple juice
- ▶ 25g/1oz sultanas

"Katie sometimes offers me some of her food – mushed up and half-chewed!"

Method

1 Preheat the oven to 180°C/350°F/Gas Mark 4 and cover two large baking trays with non-stick baking paper or parchment.

2 Sift the flour into a large mixing bowl. Add the butter and rub into the flour using your fingertips, until the mixture looks like fine breadcrumbs. Alternatively, use a food processor.

3 Add the apple juice and sultanas and mix to form a stiff dough. Bring together into a ball and roll out on a well-floured work surface to around 3mm/⅛in thick.

4 To cut into biscuits, either use a small round (or shaped) cutter, and then re-roll the remaining dough, or use a knife and cut the dough into squares or rectangles.

5 Transfer the biscuits to the prepared baking trays and bake for 12–15 minutes until they feel lightly firm. Cool fully before eating.

These delicious, lightly spiced muffins are naturally sweet, with all the sweetness coming from the pineapple, carrots and apple. They can also be made as mini-muffins, which are perfect to take out and about as a snack. They freeze well, too, defrosting in 4–6 hours at room temperature.

Carrot & pineapple muffins

Makes 12 standard-sized muffins or 20 mini-muffins

Ingredients

- ▶ A little oil or unsalted butter, for greasing
- ▶ 100ml/4fl oz sunflower oil
- ▶ 2 large eggs, beaten
- ▶ 1 tsp vanilla extract
- ▶ 250g/9oz self-raising flour
- ▶ 1 tsp baking powder
- ▶ 1 tsp ground cinnamon
- ▶ ½ tsp ground nutmeg
- ▶ 150g/5oz carrot, peeled and grated
- ▶ 135g/4½oz drained weight crushed pineapple in juice
- ▶ 75g/3oz sultanas
- ▶ 100g/4oz sugar-free apple purée (preferably home-made)
- ▶ Zest of 1 large orange, finely grated

Method

1 Preheat the oven to 180°C/350°F/Gas Mark 4 and grease a 12- or 20-hole silicone muffin tin (or line a metal muffin tin with paper cases).

2 Put the oil, eggs and vanilla into a jug and whisk. Sift the flour, baking powder, cinnamon and nutmeg into a large mixing bowl.

3 Add the carrot, pineapple, sultanas, apple purée and orange zest, and stir. Pour in the oil, egg and vanilla mixture and stir gently (or fold) until the flour is just combined (avoid over-mixing, which will make the muffins tough).

4 Spoon the mixture evenly into the muffin tin and bake for 20–25 minutes (14–18 minutes for mini-muffins) until the muffins are risen and a rich, golden brown and springy to the touch. Remove from the oven and cool on a wire rack. Serve slightly warm or cold.

These wonderfully tasty savoury muffins are a perfect match for soup and make a great alternative to sandwiches for snacks and lunchboxes. They also freeze extremely well – just take them out of the freezer in the morning and they'll be defrosted and ready to eat by lunchtime. If you want, you can make them as mini-muffins, so that you don't have to break them to share with your baby.

Cheddar & sweetcorn muffins

Makes 12 standard-sized muffins or 20 mini-muffins

Ingredients

- A little oil or unsalted butter, for greasing
- 300g/11oz self-raising flour
- 125g/4½oz Cheddar cheese, grated
- 100g/4oz sweetcorn kernels (no added salt)
- 65g/2½oz unsalted butter, melted
- 300ml/11fl oz whole milk
- 1 large egg, beaten
- 1 tsp mustard, optional

Method

1 Preheat the oven to 200°C/390°F/Gas Mark 6 and grease a 12- or 20-hole silicone muffin tin with a little oil (or line a metal muffin tin with paper cases).

2 Sift the flour into a large mixing bowl. Stir in the cheese and sweetcorn.

3 Put the melted butter, milk, egg and mustard (if using) into another mixing bowl. Stir well until evenly combined and then pour into the cheese and sweetcorn. Stir well, until all the dry ingredients are incorporated.

4 Spoon the mixture into the muffin tin, ensuring it's divided evenly. Transfer to the oven and bake for 20–25 minutes (15–18 minutes for mini-muffins), until they are well risen, a rich, golden brown, and springy to the touch. Allow to cool fully before eating.

These muffins are very versatile. They're ideal as a snack, for taking out – or even as a quick breakfast – because they freeze so well. Just take a few out of the freezer before you go to bed, leave at room temperature and they'll be defrosted by the morning.

Fruit & oat muffins

Makes 12 standard-sized muffins or 20 mini-muffins

Ingredients

- ▶ A little oil or unsalted butter, for greasing
- ▶ 200g/7oz self-raising flour
- ▶ 1 tsp baking powder
- ▶ 50g/2oz porridge oats
- ▶ 250ml/9fl oz whole milk
- ▶ 50g/2oz caster sugar or 2½ tbsp agave syrup
- ▶ 1 large egg
- ▶ 50ml/2fl oz sunflower oil or 10g/½oz unsalted butter, melted and cooled
- ▶ 175g/6oz prepared fruit

.... **TIP** ....

Mix and match the fruit you use: mixed frozen berries or small chunks of peeled and cored apple, pear, peach, plum or apricot all work well.

The recipe has a small amount of sugar/agave syrup, but you may want to experiment without any.

Method

1 Preheat the oven to 180°C/350°F/Gas Mark 4 and grease a 12- or 20-hole silicone muffin tin (or line a metal muffin tin with paper cases).

2 Put the flour into a large mixing bowl, add the baking powder and porridge oats and stir well to combine.

3 Put the milk, sugar or syrup, egg and oil into a large jug and whisk together thoroughly. Pour the mixture into the bowl containing the dry ingredients and add the fruit. Stir gently to combine.

4 When all the dry ingredients have been incorporated, spoon the mixture evenly into the muffin tin.

5 Bake for 25–30 minutes (15–18 minutes for mini-muffins) until the muffins are a rich golden brown in colour and spring back when touched gently. Allow to cool fully on a wire rack before eating or freezing.

These flapjack bars are soft and full of flavour, with no added sugar. They're also firm enough to travel well and make an ideal snack to take out and about with you. They will keep for five to seven days in an airtight container.

Flapjacks

Makes 12–14 small flapjack bars

Ingredients

- 3 medium bananas
- 75g/3oz unsalted butter, melted
- 125g/4½oz pitted dates, chopped
- 50g/2oz sultanas
- 175g/6oz porridge oats

"If we're going out I take some home-made snacks with me or some fruit – now Sofia's older she gets hungrier."

Method

1 Preheat the oven to 180°C/350°F/Gas Mark 4 and line a baking tray (around 12cm x 18cm/ 5in x 7in) with non-stick baking paper.

2 Put the bananas into a large mixing bowl and mash until smooth. Add the melted butter, dates, sultanas and oats. Mix well to ensure everything is evenly combined.

3 Pour into the prepared baking tray and level off using the back of a fork or large spoon.

4 Bake for 15 minutes. Allow to cool fully in the tray, as the mixture will firm up as it cools. Cut into small bars.

Soda bread is the easiest and quickest bread to make, with no kneading or rising. This recipe makes a soft, tender, moist loaf, with enough cheese to make it more interesting than a standard loaf, while still being lower in salt than most shop-bought breads. The optional toppings provide a variety of additional tastes and textures for your baby to discover. Younger babies may find the bread easier to manage if it's lightly toasted.

Mediterranean soda bread

Makes 1 large loaf

Ingredients

For the bread:

▸ A little oil, for greasing
▸ 450g/1lb plain flour
▸ 1 tsp bicarbonate of soda
▸ 350ml/13fl oz whole milk
▸ 100g/4oz Cheddar cheese, grated

For the topping (optional) choose any of the following:

▸ 6–8 cherry tomatoes, halved
▸ 4–5 pitted olives, halved
▸ 50g/2oz mozzarella cheese

TIP

This bread is best eaten fresh, although it can be frozen. It makes a great accompaniment for soup at lunchtime.

Method

1 Preheat the oven to 180°C/350°F/Gas Mark 4 and grease a 900g/2lb loaf tin.

2 Sift the flour and bicarbonate of soda into a large mixing bowl. Pour in the milk and add the cheese. Stir quickly to incorporate all the flour, then tip the mixture into the prepared tin. Dot the topping(s) of your choice evenly over the bread and bake for 35–45 minutes until golden on top.

3 Leave to cool in the tin for 20 minutes, then transfer to a wire rack and allow to cool fully before slicing.

Delicious desserts

Many families like to round off a meal with something sweet, at least occasionally, but desserts don't have to be full of sugar to be delicious. The simplest – and healthiest – pudding you can offer is probably fresh fruit, but this section has plenty of other ideas for you, too. Some of the recipes include a little maple or agave syrup, or sugar. However, in general, babies are happy with very little sweetness, so you may prefer to let the adults add their own sugar or syrup at the table.

Most shop-bought yoghurts – especially those marketed for children – contain a great deal of added sugar. Making your own fruit yoghurt is easy, and you'll know exactly what's in it. If he's a BLW beginner, your baby may simply lick the yoghurt off his fingers – or see page 16 for some other tips on offering runny foods.

Fresh fruit yoghurt

Serves 1 adult, 1 small child, 1 baby

Ingredients
- ▶ 150g/6oz yoghurt, preferably live, either full-fat or Greek
- ▶ 40–60g/1oz fresh fruit

Variation
For a quicker option, which will keep for a couple of days in a covered container in the fridge, use sugar-free shop-bought fruit purée. Apple, pear, peach and mango are good choices, either on their own or in combinations.

Method

1 Ensure that any fresh fruit is washed and peeled, if necessary, and that cores and stones are removed. Then mash, slice or cut into chunks to suit your baby.

To serve
Stir the prepared fruit into the yoghurt and serve immediately.

TIP
Fresh-fruit yoghurt doesn't keep well, so it needs to be eaten immediately. You can use whatever fresh fruit you have available: banana, blueberry, peeled pear, grated apple, strawberry, raspberry, peeled mango or peeled peach are all delicious choices.

You can make a very simple alternative to ice cream just by mashing some bananas and freezing them (banana never goes completely solid) but, if you want something closer to real ice cream, this refreshing frozen-yoghurt dessert is much healthier than most commercial ice creams and is quick and simple to make.

Banana ice cream

Serves a family of 6

Ingredients
- 4 very ripe bananas
- 150g/5oz full-fat natural yoghurt
- 50g/2oz caster sugar
- A couple of drops of vanilla extract

"Zara wanted to use a spoon from about 9 months and I'd help her load it up. Before long she was doing it herself."

Method

1 Put all the ingredients into a blender and whizz until smooth (or use a jug and a stick-blender).

2 Transfer the mixture to a sealable freezer-safe tub, with room for it to expand slightly, and freeze. It should take around 3 hours to freeze fully.

3 Remove the tub from the freezer about 30 minutes before serving, so that the ice cream will be soft enough to scoop.

To serve
Serve on its own or with fresh or baked fruit, fruit salad or a warm pudding.

Apple is traditionally cooked with blackberries, but you can use any type or combination of sweet berries for this dish, and defrosted frozen berries are fine, too. The oats and almonds make a nice alternative to a flour-based crumble topping and the optional vanilla and cinnamon add a delicious, subtle layer of flavour. Your baby may enjoy grabbing handfuls of this dish.

Apple & berry crumble

Serves a family of 6, generously

Ingredients

For the filling:
- 350g/12oz prepared weight of apples (peeled if wished), with cores removed, cubed
- 250g/9oz berries
- 2½ tbsp maple syrup or 50g/2oz caster sugar (or less)
- 1 tsp vanilla extract (optional)
- 1 tsp ground cinnamon (optional)

For the topping:
- 175g/6oz porridge oats
- 100g/4oz ground almonds
- 75g/3oz unsalted butter, cut into small cubes

TIPS

This crumble keeps well in the fridge for up to three days.

Using dessert apples rather than cooking apples will mean that the dish is less likely to need sweetening.

Method

1 Preheat the oven to 180°C/350°F/Gas Mark 4. Arrange the fruit evenly in the bottom of a large baking dish, approximately 20cm/8in, round or square. Drizzle the syrup (or sprinkle the sugar) and sprinkle with the vanilla and cinnamon, if using.

2 Put the oats, almonds and butter into a bowl. Rub the butter into the dry ingredients with your fingertips, to form a rough mixture. Alternatively, use a food processor.

3 Sprinkle the topping over the fruit and bake for 25–30 minutes until the filling is bubbling and the topping is lightly browned. Allow the crumble to cool for at least 30 minutes before serving.

To serve

Serve warm or cold, with cream, home-made custard or Banana ice cream (see page 171).

This is a hearty, traditional pudding that is delicious warm or cold. Although sprinkling a little caster sugar on top of the pudding just before baking will give it a nice, slightly crunchy, texture, it's not essential if you prefer to keep the dish as low-sugar as possible. You may want to sprinkle sugar on part of the pudding, leaving the rest without, for your baby.

Bread & butter pudding

Serves a family of 6–8

Ingredients

- 35g/1½oz unsalted butter, softened
- 8 slices bread (white works slightly better than brown)
- 300ml/11fl oz double cream
- 250ml/9fl oz whole milk
- 1 tsp vanilla extract
- Zest of 1 orange
- 3 large eggs, beaten
- 1 tsp cinnamon
- 1¼ tbsp maple syrup or 25g/1oz caster sugar
- 75g/3oz sultanas
- A little caster sugar for sprinkling on top (optional)

TIPS

Dry, slightly stale, bread works better than fresh bread in this recipe.

Once baked, the pudding will keep for three days in the fridge.

Method

1 Preheat the oven to 180°C/350°F/Gas Mark 4. Butter the slices of bread evenly. Cut off the crusts and cut each slice in half diagonally, to form two large triangles.

2 Pour the cream, milk, vanilla, orange zest, eggs, cinnamon and maple syrup or sugar into a large jug and whisk well.

3 Lay the buttered-bread triangles in a 1.25 litre/2 pint-capacity pudding dish, overlapping them and sprinkling on the sultanas as you go. Putting the sultanas between the slices will help them soften as they cook.

4 Pour the mixture from the jug evenly over the bread, sprinkle a little extra sugar on top, if you wish, then bake for 30–40 minutes until the surface is a rich brown colour and crispy around the edges. Allow the pudding to cool a little before serving.

A fruit salad will give your baby plenty of opportunity to pick up different shapes and is a great way to help the whole family get their five-a-day. Choose from three different delicious fruit combinations – or invent your own.

Fresh fruit salad

Serves a family of 4

Ingredients

Strawberry, pineapple and blueberry:

▸ 200g/7oz strawberries, hulled and halved

▸ ½ pineapple, skin and core removed and cut into cubes

▸ 100g/4oz ripe blueberries (larger ones halved)

▸ Juice of ½ lemon/lime

Pineapple, mango and kiwi:

▸ ½ pineapple, skin and core removed, cut into cubes

▸ 1 mango, peeled, stone removed, cut into cubes

▸ 2 kiwis, peeled, cut into slices

▸ Juice of ½ lemon/lime

Peach, raspberry and blueberry:

▸ 4–6 ripe peaches, stones removed, peeled and cut into chunks

▸ 75g/3oz raspberries

▸ 75g/3oz ripe blueberries (larger ones halved)

▸ Juice of ½ lemon/lime

Method

1 Put all the fruit into a bowl and stir. Squeeze or pour the lemon or lime juice over the top.

To serve

Serve either as it is or with plain yoghurt, cream or Banana ice cream (see page 171).

TIP

If you prefer a salad with more liquid you can cover the fruit with orange or apple juice instead of the lemon or lime..

"Aisha completely focuses on what she's doing – she's so happy exploring the food."

Baking enhances the natural sweetness of plums, peaches and nectarines, as well as making them softer, so this is a particularly good way of preparing fruit that may otherwise be a bit too firm for your baby to manage easily.

Baked fruit with vanilla & cinnamon

Serves a family of 4–6

Ingredients

▶ Approx. 450g/1lb sweet plums, peaches or nectarines

▶ 1 tsp cinnamon

▶ 1 tsp vanilla extract

▶ A little maple syrup or caster sugar (optional)

TIP

Baked fruit keeps well in the fridge in a covered container for up to five days.

Method

1 Preheat the oven to 170°C/340°F/Gas Mark 3. Halve the fruit and remove the stones. Put the fruit, cinnamon, vanilla extract and syrup or sugar (if using) into a bowl and stir gently to coat the pieces.

2 Lay the fruit pieces out, cut side up, on a large baking tray. Bake for around 20 minutes until soft.

To serve

Serve warm or cold, with plain yoghurt, cream or Banana ice cream (see page 171).

"I thought plums would be too sharp without sugar but Lena seems to love them."

This rice pudding is a rich, creamy, comforting dessert, made with coconut milk. It takes just a couple of minutes to prepare and can then be left to cook in the oven.

Rice pudding

Serves a family of 6, generously

Ingredients

- ▷ A little unsalted butter
- ▷ 1 x 400ml/14oz tin coconut milk
- ▷ 800ml/1pt 7fl oz whole milk
- ▷ 2½ tbsp maple syrup or 50g/2oz caster sugar (optional)
- ▷ 250g/9oz pudding rice

TIPS

This pudding will keep for up to three days in the fridge.

If you're planning to serve it with naturally sweet fruit or jam, you'll probably want to leave out the maple syrup or sugar (adults can add a little at the table if they want their portion sweeter).

Method

1 Preheat the oven to 140°C/280°F/Gas Mark 2 and butter the base and sides of a 2- to 3-litre ovenproof dish.

2 Whisk the coconut milk and milk together in a large mixing jug. Add the syrup or sugar (if using) and rice, and stir well. Pour into the prepared dish and stir once more.

3 Bake for 1 hour and 20–30 minutes, until the rice is cooked through.

To serve

Serve warm or cold, with fresh fruit slices, such as strawberry, mango or banana, fresh berries, stewed fruit, or a little sugar-free jam.

These crèpes are delicious, and because they can be rolled quite tightly, they're perfect for little hands to hold. Plus, freshly made fruit purée makes a quick and healthy alternative to sugary fillings.

Crèpes with fresh fruit purée

Makes 10 large crèpes – enough for a family of 4–6

Ingredients
For the batter:
- 200g/7oz plain flour
- 400ml/14oz whole milk
- 2 large eggs
- 20g/1oz unsalted butter, melted

For the fruit purée:
- 2 medium eating apples or pears, or 1 medium apple/pear and a small handful of berries, such as strawberries, raspberries or blueberries

> ## TIPS
>
> The crèpe batter can be prepared in advance and stored in the fridge for up to 4 hours before cooking. Just give it a whisk and allow it to come to room temperature before using.
>
> If you are pushed for time, you can use sugar-free shop-bought fruit purée.

Method

1 Wash all the fruit. Peel, core and slice the apples or pears. Put them in a pan with just enough water to cover them, bring to the boil and simmer for 15–20 minutes until soft. Drain off the water, add the berries (if using) and mash or blend until smooth.

2 Sift the flour into a large mixing bowl and make a well. Put the milk and eggs into a large jug and whisk. Pour the mixture into the flour and whisk until smooth. Pour the batter back into the jug, so you can measure out small amounts at a time, or use a ladle.

3 Melt the butter in a non-stick frying pan over a moderate to high heat, swirling it around until it starts to bubble. Pour in just enough batter to cover the pan base. Allow to cook for 30–45 seconds, then lift the edge to check the colour. Flip when the underside is lightly browned and cook for another 20–30 seconds on the other side.

4 Transfer the cooked crèpe to a plate, spread the purée over and roll it up. Cut to a suitable length for your baby before serving.

Recipes to take out or freeze

Life with a young family can be hectic, so we've included some recipes to help you stay on top of things. Some are dishes that can be frozen, then reheated when you're short of time, and some are foods that are good for taking out and about, so you can offer your baby healthy snacks and dishes on the go.

Recipes suitable for freezing are shown with this symbol ❄ on the recipe page; those suitable for taking out are marked with ☀ .

Food to take out

Recipe	Page
Fruity porridge fingers	43
Sweet potato falafel	58
Creamy ham & pea pasta	62
Mackerel, broccoli & couscous salad	63
Spinach & goat's cheese frittata	64
Jerk chicken drumsticks	93
Simple guacamole	112
Roasted vegetable kebabs	113
Potato salad	129
Pesto pasta with green beans	134
Chicken drumsticks	141
Wholemeal soda-bread rolls	152
Banana bread	153
No-salt flatbread	154
Easy fruit loaf	156
Cheddar & spinach scones	157
Mini-quiches	158
Wholemeal sultana scones	160
Apple biscuits	161
Carrot & pineapple muffins	163
Cheddar & sweetcorn muffins	164
Fruit & oat muffins	165
Flapjacks	166
Mediterranean soda bread	167

Dishes for freezing

Index

Acknowledgements

We would like to say a huge thank you to all the people who have helped to make this book possible. Firstly, thank you to all the mums, dads and babies who gave up their time to talk to us about their experiences of baby-led weaning or to have their pictures taken to illustrate the book: Emily Ackroyd and Rosa and Rafe Ackroyd-Todd, Bronwyn Ashby and Florence and Niall Lewis, Melanie Edwards and Jude Edwards, Ruth Fisher and Hetty Radford, Sarah Meagher Gaymer and Nate Gaymer, Laura and Luke Hastings and Josiah and Ariana Hastings, Sarah-Jane Hurst and Rory Hurst, Zainab Lantan and Junior Lantan, Ela Law, Milly Law and William Law, Ria Mamujee-Towers and Ari Mamujee-Towers, Samantha Walsham and Jack Walsham, Rachel Walters and Toby McLeod, and Siobhan Watts and Rory Calder Watts, Roxanna Whittaker, Meredith Whittaker and Benedict Whittaker. We only wish we'd had room to use all the quotes and tips you provided.

We also want to thank Charlotte Pike for her patience, resourcefulness and kitchen know-how, Isabel de Cordova (www.isabeldecordova.com) for the use of her pottery in the photographs, and our fantastic production team: Jo Godfrey Wood and Peggy Sadler of Bookworx, for editing and design, and Ruth Jenkinson (and her assistant Julie Stewart) for photography. We're grateful to Laura Herring for proofreading and to Marie Lorimer for taking care of the index. Finally, our thanks go to our editor, Katy Denny, who coordinated the whole process, and to our agent, Clare Hulton, who continues to support us to share our knowledge and ideas. And, as always, thanks to our families and friends for their thoughtful feedback.

Check out our first recipe book, *The Baby-led Weaning Cookbook: 180 delicious recipes for the whole family to enjoy*, for lots more recipes for you and your baby.